D0371449

Michał Rożek

Cracow

City of Kings

Photos:
Janusz Podlecki

© GeoCenter Warszawa,
  Division of Bertelsmann Media Sp. z o.o. 1996
© RV Reise-und Verkehrsverlag, München 1996
© Geo Data geographishe Datenbanken GmbH & Co KG,
  Stuttgart, Berlin, Hamburg, Potsdam, Leipzig 1996

Cover photo: Cathedral on Wawel Hill, Janusz Podlecki, Cracow
Photos: Janusz Podlecki, Cracow

Author: Michał Rożek, Cracow
English translation: Birgit Helen Beile, Münster
Idea and series conception: Prisma Verlag GmbH, Munich
Editing, coordination: Prisma Verlag GmbH, Munich

Type-setting: Buchmacher Bär, Freising
Reproduction: Printex, Verona
Cover layout: Prisma Verlag GmbH, Munich

ISBN 83-86146-71-0

Contents

Map of the town centre 8

Town History 10

Walk: The King's Way 34

Walk: Wawel Hill 58

Walk: Kazimierz 74

Excursions 86

General map 88

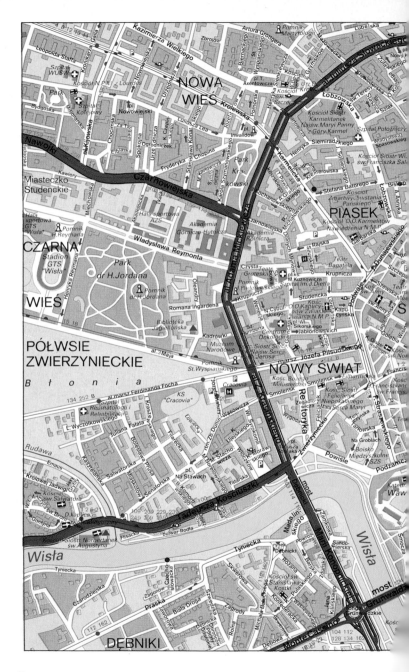

9

Above: Miniature from the Codex of Balthasar Behem, 16th c.
Page 2: The towers of the Church of Our Lady.
Page 6/7: View of the Wawel, seen from the Weichsel.

Town History

 Centuries ago Cracow, the town on the Vistula river, was already called »*totius Poloniae urbs celeberrima*«, which means »the most famous town in Poland«. And this is still the case. Cracow owes its fame mainly to its long and varied history, which is reflected in the name of this old royal town. Cracow is a town with a turbulent history that represents the Polish national identity in a particular way. According to legend the name of the town derives from the mythical Prince Krak who is said to have founded the settlement at the foot of Wawel Hill.

Cracow's origins lie hidden in the darkness of time, as archaeological examinations have shown. The town's two artificial hills *Krakus* and *Wanda*, which date from the early Middle Ages (7th–8th c.) and are named after two legendary rulers of Cracow, seem to confirm the origins of the former capital of Poland. The earliest mention of Cracow dates from the year 965, from the time when Mieszko I and with him the whole of Poland accepted baptism and were therefore allowed to feel part of the family of the Christian European countries. Towards the end of the tenth century Cracow was annexed to the Piast state. One mute witness to those troubled times is the stone rotunda of the Chapel of Our Lady (second half of the 10th c., later known as the Rotunda of St Felix and Adauctus), which stands on Wawel Hill. Archaeological excavations have shown that other sacral buildings stood next to it on the Wawel.

In the year 1000 a bishopric, subordinated to the archbishopric of Gnesen, was founded in Cracow. For this reason several new Romanesque buildings were erected on Wawel Hill, which from the mid-eleventh century on was to become the seat of government for many centuries. Amongst these buildings mention should be made of the so-called First Wawel Cathedral, which was built by Bolesław Chrobry/Boleslav the Brave. In time Cracow achieved a leading position amongst the Polish towns. Under Duke Kazimierz Odnowiciel/Casimir the Restorer (1040–1058) Cracow first took on the function of a capital, and indeed remained the official capital of the extensive state until the end of the eighteenth century, i.e. until the decline of the Polish state. The coronation treasure was kept on the Wawel, and a well-known cathedral school was founded here in the eleventh century, whose graduates either became churchmen or »civil servants«. In the second half of the eleventh century Cracow was witness to a tragedy of serious consequence, when King Bolesław Śmiały/Boleslav the Fearless had Abbot Stanisław Szczepanowski executed in the year 1079. The king was banned from Poland and the crown was lost for over 200 years.

At the beginning of the twelfth century Cracow was an imposing and well-populated town. Above the town there towered the Wawel, on which a fortified castle and several churches stood in addition to the stone-built so-called Second Wawel Cathedral, which had been erected in Romanesque style by Duke Władysław Herman. To the north of the Wawel the foundations of the present town centre of Cracow, known as Okół, were established. Amongst the larger sacral edifices erected here were the Romanesque St Andrew's Church (11th–12th c.), which still stands, and a little later the churches of St Martin and St Mary Magdalene. On the site of the present market square there stood the little Romanesque Church of św. Wojciech/St Adalbert, on which building work was begun as early as the tenth century. In the twelfth century there followed the Romanesque Salvator Church as well as the Romanesque churches of św. Mikolaj/St Nicolas and St Florian. The so-called *Statut Krzywoustego*/Statute of King Boleslav Squintmouth, the so-called seniority statute, dating from 1138, which concerns the line of succession in Poland, named Cracow as the capital of the seniority territory and secured the ruler over Little Poland and Cracow the position of Grandduke (i.e. the seniority) over other parts of Poland. From this time on Cracow had the function of a capital during a period in which Poland was divided into different principalities; however it was also the object of perpetual argument as these individual principalities debated over the line of succession.

In the year 1241 Cracow was destroyed in the Mongol invasion, which has traditionally been called the Tartar invasion. In 1257 the town was faced with a considerable task concerning both town planning and jurisprudence. Based on the town rights of Wrocław/Breslau and using the Magdeburg Rights as a model, Prince Bolesław Wstydliwy/Boleslav the Chaste awarded Cracow the location privilege. Every visitor to Cracow is astounded at the logic and precision as well as the structure of the whole town

Coronation sword of the Polish kings.

complex, which is particularly visible in the market square and the geometrical road system, into which the Romanesque buildings were integrated. Cracow's market square is considered one of the most important town planning solutions and is as attractive as the Square of San Marco in Venice or St Peter's Square in the Vatican.

The awarding of the location privilege marked the beginning of a period in which medieval art blossomed in Cracow and became a credit to the town. With the help of the privilege from Prince Leszek Czarny/Leszek the Black, the project of surrounding the town with homogeneously built fortifications was begun after the year 1285. The building work continued until the end of the Middle Ages. You can still see remains of the defence walls at the

13

Part of the tomb of King Władisław Jagiełło.

Brama Floriańska/St Florian's Gate and at the Barbican. Unfortunately the remainder of the walls were torn down at the beginning of the nineteenth century and replaced by the *Planty*/parks, which form a green girdle around the town centre. Today they form one of Cracow's main attractions.

Since the fourteenth century, i.e. after the union of the Polish state under the rule of King Władysław Łokietek/Ladislav the Short, Cracow has been the coronation town of the Polish kings as well as their place of burial. The first monarch to be crowned on the Wawel was Władysław Łokietek/Ladislav the Short, who died in 1333. In fact it was the crowning of Ladislav the Short in 1320 that finally decided on Cracow's status of capital within the Polish kingdom, which had been reformed after its division into small principalities. Władysław Łokietek was also the first king to be buried in Wawel Cathedral. During this period the old Romanesque cathedral gave way to a Gothic church building (1320–1364), which has remained standing up to the present day and is the most impressive historical architectural monument in Poland, a true treasure chamber of national culture.

During the reign of the last Piast ruler King Kazimierz Wielki/Casimir the Great (died 1370), the son of Łokietek, who was a generous patron of the arts, a supporter of the sciences and a skilful administrator, Cracow developed further. Close to his capital Casimir the Great founded the »satellite« towns of Kazi-

14

Altar by Veit Stoß in the Church of Our Lady.

mierz (1335) and Kleparz (1366), which in the course of time were integrated into the town of Cracow.

King Casimir gave Cracow many privileges, which contributed to the economic upswing of the town, though this was in any case favoured by Cracow's geographical location at the crossing point of trade routes. The second half of the 14th century saw the erection of monumental sacral edifices, such as the Church of Our Lady on the *Rynek Główny*/Market Square or the churches of St Catherine and *Bożego Ciała*/Corpus Christi in Kazimierz.

View of Cracow from Schedel's »Chronicle of the World«, 1493.

To Casimir the Great, Poland also owes the foundation of a
university in the year 1364. The lack of educated legal advisers and
physicians had long been felt in the Polish kingdom, and these
needs could only be fulfilled by a university. After Prague
University, which was founded in 1348, the Cracow »High
School« was the second in Central Europe.

The powerful King Casimir was the last Piast king to rule
Poland. In accordance with contemporary treaties, Hungarian
kings from the house of Anjou assumed the rule over the kingdom
of Poland: King Ludwig (1370–1382) and his daughter
Jadwiga/Hedwig (1384–1399). 1385 was the year of the Polish-
Lithuanian Union in Krewo. The Grand Prince of Lithuania,

Jagiełło, received the hand of the young Jadwiga in marriage and thereby also the Polish throne; he had himself baptised and assumed the name of Władysław/Ladislav. Thus Cracow became the capital of the extensive Jagiellon empire, which encompassed White Ruthenia and Lithuania as well as ethnically Polish regions.

As a consequence of generous legacies by Jadwiga and the efforts of Władysław Jagiełło the university, at which students are taught to this day, was restored in the year 1400. Cracow University, which was called the Cracow Academy at the time, took an active part in the councils of the first half of the fifteenth century. It was an excellent school of political thought; the name of Paweł Włodkowic, whose erudition was remarked upon during the

Council in Constance, comes to mind. At the end of the fifteenth century the Alma Mater was attaining fame through many of its graduates; especially through Mikołaj Kopernik/Nicolaus Copernicus, who studied the fundamental principles of mathematics and astronomy here. The picturesque building of the Collegium Maius was erected towards the end of the fifteenth century at the request of the professors from the High School; today it houses the Museum of the Jagiellonian University.

The political stability after the Peace of Toruń/Thorn (1466), which ended the war with the Knights of the Cross, furthered Cracow's economic and cultural development. This upswing was also aided by the patronage of King Kasimierz Jagiellończyk/ Casimir the Jagiellon (1447–1492) and Elisabeth of Habsburg as well as by the prosperity of the middle classes. The town also became a significant centre of humanistic thought; its eminent scholars included Filippo Buonaccorsi, called Callimachus, who had come from far-off Italy, and the humanistic writer Conrad Celtis, who lived here for about two years. Like the historian Jan Długosz, Callimachus was tutor to the royal children. During this time, namely in 1473, the first book to be printed in Poland was published in Cracow.

The end of the fifteenth century also saw the creative period of the finest medieval sculptor, Master Veit Stoß, who came here from Nuremberg in 1477 as he had been commissioned by the inhabitants of Cracow to carve the high altar for the Church of Our Lady. He also created the tombstone of King Kazimierz Jagiellończyk, a stone crucifix for the Church of Our Lady, and the design of the memorial slab for said Fillipo Callimachus. Another building complex erected at the end of the fifteenth century was the Barbican, one of the few examples of its kind in Europe.

During the same period a Jewish quarter developed in Kazimierz, which for centuries proved fascinating due to its unique atmosphere and its own culture. Several synagogues were erected here in the sixteenth century, amongst them the Old Synagogue and the Remu'h Synagogue with the Old Jewish Cemetery.

The so-called »Golden Age« was the time of Cracow's greatest splendour. The last of the Jagiellons were ruling on the Wawel: Zygmunt I Stary/Sigismund I the Old (died 1548) and his son Zygmunt August/Sigismund Augustus (died 1572). At the time the first examples of Renaissance art were being created, for example, in the cathedral the memorial slab of King Jan Olbracht/John Albert. Located in an arcade of double pilasters, it was created by the Italian architect and sculptor Francesco Fiorentino in the early

Cracow's old coat of arms from the Codex of Balthasar Behem.

sixteenth century. The king had the medieval Wawel Castle turned into a magnificent Renaissance palace; modelled on Italian examples, its centre is formed by an arcaded courtyard. The rebuilding work was overseen by Francesco Fiorentino and, after his death, by Master Benedikt from Sandomierz, followed by

Cracow panorama – Braun-Hogenberg, »Civitates Orbis Terrarum«

20

Bartolomeo Berecci. Sigismund I the Old commissioned Berecci to build the Sigismund Chapel (1519–1531), the most outstanding example of Renaissance architecture in Poland. Visitors to Cracow have referred to it as »the pearl of the Renaissance north of the Alps«. The Sigismund Chapel is the resting place of the last Jagiellons. Soon after it was built both ecclesiastical and secular dignitaries followed the example of their monarch and had chapels resembling the Sigismund Chapel built – first onto Wawel Cathedral and later onto other Polish churches.

Of the political events of the time the famous Prussian Vow of Allegiance (1525), which was given on the market square in Cracow, should be mentioned. Albrecht of Brandenburg, the last grand master of the Knights of the Cross, and after his conversion to the Lutheran faith the first secular duke of Prussia, vowed feudal allegiance to Sigismund I the Old. From that time on the Duchy of Prussia, the former state of the Knights of the Cross, belonged to the kingdom of Poland and the Order of the Knights of the Cross was secularized.

King Zygmunt August/Sigismund Augustus ordered an unusual collection of tapestries as decoration for Wawel Palace. These tapestries were woven in the best workshops in Brussels. Though the collection was decimated in the course of the centuries, it still forms the centre-piece of the art collections on the Wawel and bears testimony to the artistic taste of a monarch who in the role of a patron of the arts had no cause to fear comparison with other contemporary European kings.

The death of Sigismund Augustus in 1572 marked the end of the Jagiellon dynasty, and a period of elected kingship began for the union of Poland and Lithuania. Cracow remained the capital of the kingdom, though political life was gradually being transferred to Warsaw. As a consequence, Cracow, though officially the capital, lost much of its importance to Warsaw.

The Cracow of the Renaissance period consisted not only of the royal court on the Wawel, but also of the raucous, pulsating life of the actual town of Cracow. Wealthy patrician families, the Kaufmanns, Betmans and Boners, donated pieces of art that were mainly designated for the Church of Our Lady. In this church you will find art objects of a high quality, for example by Hans Süß of Kulmbach and Gian Maria Padovano. On account of the trade links with Nuremberg, examples of Nuremberg art also found their way to Cracow. The patrician Seweryn Boner commissioned from the Vischers a bronze tombstone for himself and his wife Zofia née Betman for the family chapel in the Church of Our Lady. After a

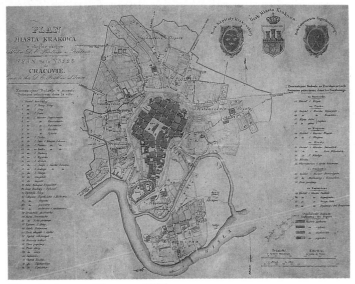

Historical map of Cracow, 1836.

fire in the year 1555 the old Gothic cloth halls were rebuilt in Renaissance style by the Italian Master Pankracy, Gian Maria Padovano and Santi Gucci. The burgher houses were also rebuilt and turned into virtual palaces.

In the sixteenth century Polish culture attained European standard, and formed links especially with the countries of the German empire and with Italy. Cracow became a cultural centre famous for its wealth of art treasures, which were located in churches and private houses. At the foot of the Wawel the famous poets Mikołaj Rej and Jan Kochanowski were writing their works. During this period Cracow became one of the leading centres of the Reformation; Faustus Socinus, famous throughout the whole of Europe, lived and worked here.

The seventeenth century marked the beginning of a new chapter of art and culture in Cracow. Until the middle of the following century the Baroque style, which had been imported from Rome, dominated exclusively. King Zygmunt III. Waza/ Sigismund III Wasa, an experienced patron of the arts, was to a large extent responsible for the artistic predilections at the turn of the sixteenth century. An example of this patronage is the fact that he employed Giovanni Battista Trevano, who was responsible for the Baroque rebuilding of Wawel Palace, and who also designed the final appearance of the Jesuit Church of Sts Peter and Paul and of the mausoleum of Bishop Stanisław/Stanislas in Wawel Cathedral (two latter works have been recently attributed to M. Castello).

The Camaldolese Church in Bielany was completed in the third decade of the seventeenth century. It was the work of architect Andrea Spezza, who designed this unusual edifice in the spirit of late Mannerism. The church has a lovely facade and fits beautifully into the surrounding Wolski Forest.

In the year 1609 Sigismund III left Cracow and marched towards Moscow. After he had achieved the decisive victory in the so--called Smolensk War and had captured Smolensk (1611) the monarch did not return to Cracow but established his seat in Warsaw. Though Cracow formally remained the capital of Poland, it only relived its former glory during coronation festivities or funerals. Since this time it has, however, been cast in the role of a national shrine. The Swedes destroyed the town, occupying it from 1655 to 1657. They laid waste to it, stripped the town of its art treasures, and were to return once more in 1702. After each of these occasions the town arose again, like a phoenix from the ashes.

At the end of the seventeenth century the professors from the university initiated the building of the most important edifice designed in Polish Baroque style, the St Anne's Church. It was the work of the exceptional architect Tylman van Gameren and the Italian sculptor Baldassare Fontana, who created the stucco decoration in the interior of the church. Fontana also ornamented the Romanesque interior of the St Andrew's Church and carried out stucco work in many burgher houses. In his work this artist directly followed the creations of the famous Italian Giovanni Lorenzo Bernini, the leading artist of the Roman Baroque.

In the first half of the eighteenth century Cracow's economic situation was not particularly healthy; nevertheless, several pieces of splendid architecture were created during this time. The buildings were mainly designed by two architects, by the Pole Kacper Bażanka (Missionary Church in Stradom, interior of the Piarist Church) and, after the middle of the eighteenth century, by the Italian Francesco Placidi (Church of the Hospitallers in Kazimierz and the façade of the Piarist Church). The Baroque rebuilding of the ensemble of buildings of the Pauline »Na Skałce«/»On the Rock«, carried out by the architects Anton Gerhardt Müntzer and Antoni Solari, also deserves mention.

Baroque culture formed the appearance of the town and turned Cracow into a true Baroque city. The Gothic churches were rebuilt

Detail of »Kościuszko at Racławice«, by Jan Matejko.

and furnished with new paintings, altars and sculptures. The interior of the Gothic *Bożego Ciała*/Corpus Christi Church in Kazimierz is a good example. During this period the artists Antoni Frączkiewicz, Antoni Gegenpauer and Jan and Wojciech Rojowski represented the art of sculpting in Cracow. The newly designed sacral interiors were decorated with illusionistic wall paintings by

The Dominican Church before the fire, painting by T.B. Stachowicz.

Franz Gregor Ignaz Eckstein (Piarist Church) and Joseph Piltz (Church of the Hospitallers, former Trinitarian Church), who were representatives of the art movement which had been initiated by the Italian artist Andrea del Pozzo.

Apart from Gothicism, it was the Baroque style in its Roman form that most influenced the appearance of Cracow – which at the time could bear comparison with the leading European cultural cities. The artistic landscape of the old Cracow is dominated by Baroque works of art.

In the eighteenth century, however, foreign troops passing through Cracow (e.g. from Saxony and Russia) brought destruction to the town. Further damage was caused as a result of the Confederation of Bar, concluded in the year 1768, as it gave grounds for skirmishes for possession of the town, which was continually changing owners at the time.

It was not until the last quarter of the eighteenth century that Cracow witnessed any far-reaching structural and cultural changes. The Cracow Academy was fundamentally reorganised and turned into a Royal High School. This was achieved under the direction of Hugo Kołłątaj, who worked for the Commission of National

Cracow market square in the early 19th c., by Marcin Zaleski.

Education. The Medical School was reformed and a university hospital was founded. The Botanical Gardens and an observatory also date from this time.

Cracow was also the centre of great political events. In the year 1794 the nation led by Tadeusz Kościuszko rose to the defence of the unity and independence of the state. On 24 March 1794 Kościuszko took an oath to the nation on the Cracow market square, which marked the beginning of the unsuccessful Kościuszko uprising. In the year 1795 the three nations Russia, Austria and Prussia carried out the partition of Poland. Cracow fell to Austria and remained under Habsburg rule until 1918, excepting the period of the Grand Duchy of Warsaw (1809–1812) and the Republic of Cracow (1815–1846). Very soon the town fulfilled the role of the spiritual capital of all three divided regions.

The main factor that united the divided regions during this period, which lasted for more than a century, was culture. Though it lacked freedom Cracow experienced an incredible artistic and intellectual development in the nineteenth century due to its culture. It became a place of pilgrimage for many Poles, who felt enthralled by the past within its walls. From all over the country

27

The Cloth Halls in the 19th c., before structural alteration.

people thronged to these national relics, especially during the time of the Republic of Cracow. A feeling of historical unity took hold of everyone who came to this ancient town, the former capital of the Piasts and Jagiellons. Thus a sense of Cracow's special importance for the national culture was consolidated in the whole of Poland during this period.

The Wawel continued to be used as a place of burial, and as there was a lack of kings, national heroes and later poets were also buried here. In the year 1817 Prince Józef Poniatowski was laid to rest in the subterranean vaults of the cathedral, in 1818 Tadeusz Kościuszko was buried here. Adam Mickiewicz was interred on the Wawel in 1890, and a further poet, Juliusz Słowacki, was buried here in 1927. The Kościuszko Hill was raised between 1820 and 1823; its shape is reminiscent of the two burial mounds of *Krakus* and *Wanda* from the early Middle Ages.

The revolution of 1846, which ended with the defeat of the rebels and the annexation of Cracow into the Austrian section, meant the end of the town of Cracow.

In the year 1846 the inhabitants of Cracow were once more witness to a »people's spring«, which was suppressed by the Austrians with much bloodshed. A period of Germanization and the restriction of the citizens' freedoms followed. In 1850 a fire storm destroyed a whole section of Cracow. Amongst the buildings

Market Square, 19th c.

that burnt down were the Dominican Church, the Franciscan Church and the Bishop's Palace. Priceless works of art were lost.

It was not until the second half of the nineteenth century, the time of the autonomy of Galicia, that the importance of Cracow as a centre of science and the arts increased. (The Austrian section Galicia received its own district parliament, a district committee and a governor; Polish became the official language in public institutions.) During this time several mayors, most particularly Dr Józef Dietl, laid the foundations of Cracow's development. The town was given the epithet »Athens of Poland«. The Jagiellonian University and the Academy of Science, which was founded in 1872 and united scholars from all three annexed regions, occupied a leading position in the world of learning. The Cracow intelligentsia set the tone for the whole town. The professors from the Alma Mater initiated large patriotic festivities which were talked about in the whole of Poland and which served »to glorify our ancestors, and to create hope for our brethren«, as the inscription on the plinth of the Grunwald Monument reads. In the year 1880 the crypt of the Pauline Church »*Na Skałce*«/»On the Rock« became a mausoleum for Polish citizens who had made a considerable contribution to the national culture.

The time of Galician independence was also a period of extensive town planning and architectural development in Cracow.

The architects of the town (Zygmunt Hendel, Tomasz Pryliński, Sławomir Odrzywolski, Jan Zawiejski) oriented themselves towards contemporary European architecture and erected impressive buildings. During this time a modern method of restoring buildings was developed, for which Cracow became famous. With the support of the Jagiellonian University, a Polish archaeology and art history were established. The town acquired various museum collections. In 1876 the Museum of the Czartoryski Princes was founded, containing impressive art collections including paintings by Leonardo da Vinci, Raphael and Rembrandt. The National Museum, which mainly collected Polish art, was founded in 1879. Thus Cracow became a centre of museums and private collections, and the art life in the town flourished. Neither should the impressive development of the theatre be forgotten nor the work of Jan Matejko (died 1893), whose unique paintings of historical scenes formed the Polish sense of history.

At the turn of the nineteenth century the town was dominated by an artistic group supporting the very newest art movements reaching Poland from the west. This was the time of the *Młoda Polska*/Young Poles. The following artists worked in Cracow at the time: Stanisław Wyspiański, Włodzimierz Tełmajer, Józef Mehoffer, Julian Fałat, Leon Wyczółkowski and Jacek Malczewski, to name only the most important. This group of artists gathered in the literary cabaret *Zialony Balonik*/Little Green Balloon, which was located in a pastry shop (today a café) called *Jama Michalika*/Michalik's Cave. Jan Michalik's former pastry shop, which was partly reconstructed after World War II, is to be found in Florianska Street.

On the eve of World War I Cracow became a Polish Piemont. Resistance movements were formed here, and it was from here that the divisions loyal to Józef Piłsudski went into battle to fight for the liberation of their homeland. During this period Cracow was considered to represent Polishdom as a whole.

After Poland had gained its independence in the year 1918, Cracow remained an important centre for the arts and sciences, in spite of its location on the periphery of the state. In 1919 the Mining Academy, the first technical university of its kind in Poland, was founded in Cracow, near the mining area of Upper Silesia. Both the University and also the extremely active Academy of Sciences secured the town's leading position in the sciences. After the war the restoration of the Wawel was finally completed. The royal palace was furnished and regained its former character of a royal seat.

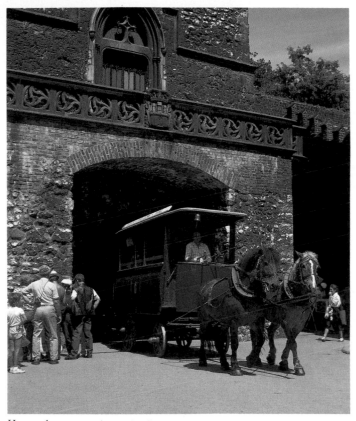

Horse-drawn carriages in Cracow

The tapestry collection of Sigismund Augustus and the royal treasure chamber, both returned by the Russians according to the treaty of Riga (1921), became the show-pieces of the collections in the palace.

The poet Juliusz Słowacki (1927) and Field Marshal Józef Piłsudski (1935) were given their last resting-place in the crypt beneath the cathedral.

The peace and the stature of this royal city were brought to an end in 1939 through Hitler's invasion of Poland and the beginning of World War II. The occupying forces were intent on brutally exterminating the intelligentsia. The Jagiellonian University was closed, the professors from the universities were arrested and deported to concentration camps. Cracow was made the headquarters of the general government. This state of affairs lasted until the January of 1945. Freedom returned then, but accompanied by a new socio-political system that the people had not wanted. Close to the old Cracow a collective metal-working combine, the so-called Lenin Works (now called after Tadeusz Sendzimir), was erected, which contributed to the ecological destruction of Cracow. The large housing estate Nowa Huta was built next to the combine in 1950. More new residential areas sprung up, which now surround the old Cracow in the form of suburbs. Unfortunately, nobody considered at the time that they would completely conceal Cracow itself.

In spite of all these changes Cracow has remained a centre of the arts and sciences. The best-known Polish composer, Krzysztof Penderecki, composes his music here; here Stanisław Lem writes his novels. And it is not long ago that Tadeusz Kantor (died 1990), who created the world-famous avant-garde theatre *Cricot 2*, worked here. The political cabaret *Piwnica Pod Baranami*/Cellar of the Rams, which is directed by Piotr Skrzynecki, has been part of Cracow's cultural scene since 1956. Cracow is a town of museums and theatres, among them the famous *Theatr Stary*/Old Theatre. In the town you will also find over a dozen colleges and universities offering a wide range of subjects.

The Cracow student Karol Wojtyła grew up in the shade of the ancient university. Formerly an actor in the underground theatre during the occupation, dramatist and poet, he later became a priest and finally bishop of Cracow, from where he was called to the Holy See in 1978 by the Sacred College. Pope John Paul II has also become a small part of the culture of contemporary Cracow.

Scores of tourists from all over the world come to the Cracow of today, wishing to get to know the town of the Pope and of Nicolaus Copernicus, the ancient capital of the Piasts and Jagiellons, the last resting place of kings and national heroes, the town that conceals priceless art treasures within its walls. This unusual and exceptional wealth was honoured in 1978 when the UNESCO included Cracow in the list of the world's cultural heritage, which bears witness to the high cultural standing of this city of kings.

The Cloth Halls.

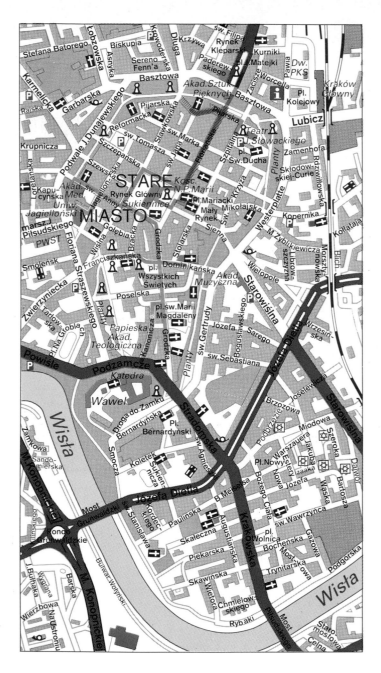

Walk
The King's Way

**Plac Matejki/Matejko Square • Pomnik
Grunwaldzki/Grunwald Monument • Barbican
Brama Floriańska/St Florian's Gate • Planty/Parks
Teatr Słowackiego/Słowacki Theatre • Kościół św.
Krzyża/Church of the Holy Cross • Czartoryski Museum
Ulica Floriańska/St Florian's Street • Jama
Michalika/Michalik's Cave • Jan Matejko House
Pharmacy Museum • Hotel Pod Różą/Rose Hotel • Rynek
Główny/Market Square • Sukiennice/Cloth Halls • Muzeum
Narodowe/National Museum • Adam Mickiewicz
Monument • Kościół Mariacki/Church of Our Lady
Kościół św. Barbary/St Barbara's Church • Houses around
the Market Square • Collegium Maius • Kościół św. Anny/
St Anne's Church • Ulica Grodzka/Grodzka Street
Dominican and Franciscan Church • Bishop's Palace
Kościół św. św. Piotra i Pawła/Church of Sts Peter and Paul
Kościół św. Andrzeja/St Andrew's Church
Ulica Kanonicza/Kanonicza Street
Stanisław Wyspiański Museum • Jan Długosz House**

This walk through Cracow begins on the **Matejko Square**. The so-called King's Way, along which the royal entourage proceeded on its way to Wawel Hill for a coronation or a funeral, began here. This was also the way that foreign envoys took. The route led from the Matejko Square through part of the town fortifications, along St Florian's Street, across the market square and through the Grodzka and Kanonicza Streets up to the Wawel, to the Cathedral or the Royal Palace. The King's Way is one of Cracow's most important tourist attractions; the historical buildings that line it are important cultural monuments.

The Matejko Square forms part of the market square of the old town of Kleparz, which was founded in the year 1366 by King Casimir the Great. A monumental equestrian statue of King

The route of the walk is marked in grey in the map opposite.

The Grunwald Monument on Matejko Square.

Władysław Jagiełło, which is called the **Grunwald Monument**, stands in the centre of the square. Erected in 1910 on the occasion of the 500th anniversary of the victory over the Knights of the Cross in the battle near Grunwald, it was donated by the famous pianist, composer and statesman Ignacy Jan Paderewski. The statue is the work of Antoni Wiwulski; also involved in its execution were Franciszek Black and Bolesław Bałzukiewicz. After being destroyed by the Nazis in 1940, the monument was reconstructed in the year 1976. Standing before it, you can see on the left the monumental building of the Academy of the Fine Arts, dating from the year 1880, with which a group of leading Polish artists was closely linked. The north side of the Matejko Square is

36

The Barbican.

formed by the St Florian's Church. In its present shape it dates from the second half of the seventeenth century, but its earlier buildings go back to medieval times. From here we come to the town fortifications.

The walls surrounding medieval Cracow were built in stages, beginning in the late thirteenth century. In the course of time this defence system was often extended. The fortifications consisted of a double wall and a broad moat. In this form they survived, though much neglected, until the beginning of the nineteenth century, when the Austrian government ordered the razing of the fortifications. This order was carried out during the existence of the Grand Duchy of Warsaw. Only the Barbican with the *Brama Floriańska*/St Florian's Gate and three bastions were saved. The Cracow **Barbican** is one of the most interesting European examples of fortification architecture. This round Gothic edifice, which is crowned by seven towers, was built between 1498 and 1499. Originally the Barbican was linked to St Florian's Gate by a so-called »throat«, which was also torn down in the first half of the nineteenth century. The whole complex was surrounded by a broad moat. The ***Brama Floriańska*/St Florian's Gate** is one of Cracow's oldest gates; it is first mentioned in documents at the beginning of the fourteenth century. Together with the Barbican it was the splendid *Porta Gloriae*/Gate of Honour through which the royal entourage entered the town. From the Barbican side you can see a coat of arms with the Piast eagle, designed by Jan Matejko, and from the St Florian's Street side a late-Baroque relief which portrays St Florian. Of the old bastions only the Passementerie Manufacturers' Bastion to the east of the gate and the Joiners' and Carpenters' Bastion to the west have been preserved. From the *Planty*/parks situated between the two bastions you can see the building of the town armoury.

When the medieval fortifications had been demolished, the area was levelled, and the walls and moats were replaced by the *Planty*/**parks**. They are nearly three kilometres long, occupy an area of approx. 21 hectares, and form a green tourist attraction. Monuments, mainly erected in the last quarter of the nineteenth century, are harmoniously integrated into the parks.

The way leads through St Florian's Gate, and then turns to the left and runs along the town wall up to *Plac św. Ducha*/Square of the Holy Ghost, where the Juliusz **Słowacki Theatre**, built by Jan Zawiejski between 1891 and 1893, is located. A statue of Aleksander Fredro von Cyprian Godebski, a writer of comedies, stands in front of the theatre. The magnificent interior contains a famous curtain that was painted by Henryk Siemiradzki in 1894. Squeezed between the Słowacki Theatre and the *Planty* stands the Gothic *Kościół św. Krzyża*/**Church of the Holy Cross**.

From here we return to St Florian's Gate. To the left you can see a charming little spot with the Joiners' Bastion, the armoury and the building complex of the **Czartoryski Museum**, which was founded at the beginning of the nineteenth century by Princess Izabela Czartoryska. The collection only came to Cracow in 1876; the museum entrance is at *Ulica św. Jana 19*/19 St John's Street. In addition to national devotional objects, this extremely valuable collection contains extensive holdings of classical and medieval art as well as paintings by Italian, Flemish and Dutch masters, for example Leonardo da Vinci's »Lady with Ermine« and Rembrandt's »Landscape with the Good Samaritan«.

Adjacent to the museum you can see the eighteenth-century Piarist Church, designed by Kacper Bażanka, with a facade by Francesco Placidi. The interior is adorned with illusionistic wall paintings by Franz Gregor Ignaz Eckstein.

The *Ulica Floriańska*/**St Florian's Street** is one of Cracow's main streets. House No. 45 is the former pastry shop of Jan Apolinary Michalik from Lemberg, which everyone called *Jama Michalika*/**Michalik's Cave** and which was a meeting-place for artists at the beginning of this century. The »Little Green Balloon«

Das Florianstor.

39

cabaret (with a satirical puppet show) was founded here in 1905. The interior, which was designed by Karol Frycz and is typical of the art of the *Młoda Polska*/Young Poles, has been preserved.

A little further along we come to No. 41, the **Jan Matejko House**, which now is a museum to this great Polish painter of historical scenes, who was born here in 1838 and died in the same house in 1893. The house No. 25 is the **Pharmacy Museum** of the Cracow Medical Academy. The history of pharmacies in Poland from the Middle Ages to the 20th century is shown here in systematic order. This museum can be compared to similar institutions in Basel and Heidelberg. Walking further along St Florian's Street you come to the impressive building No. 14, the famous **Rose Hotel**. Tsar Alexander I and the composer Franz Liszt stayed here in the last century. It is said that the French writer Honoré de Balzac also stayed here, but research has now shown that this was not the case. A lovely Renaissance portal forms the hotel entrance. We are now gradually approaching the market square. On the left hand side you can see the house No. 13, an early-Renaissance palace which belonged to the Kmita family at the beginning of the sixteenth century.

Cracow's **market square** is one of the largest squares in Europe. It was created on an area of four hectares at the time when Cracow was awarded the location privilege (1257). For many centuries it formed the centre of social, commercial and religious life and was also the place of executions. The market square has been a witness to many historical events, such as the Prussian Vow of Allegiance (1525) and the oath of Tadeusz Kościuszko (1794). These events are commemorated by plaques inserted into the cobblestones. In the centre of the square stand the ***Sukiennice*/Cloth Halls**, i.e. old »general stores« that were built as early as the Middle Ages. They were refashioned in the second half of the sixteenth century, when master builders Pankracy, Gian Maria Padovano and Santi Gucci rebuilt them after a fire. The attica with the characteristic mascarons (the work of Santi Gucci), which crowns the building, also dates from this period. The loggias, which are supported by columns, were designed by Gian Maria Padovano. The Gothic arcades, which run along the length of the building, and the protruding facade bays, on the other hand, were added between 1875 and 1879 according to designs by Tomasz Pryliński. Jan Matejko helped Pryliński with the rebuilding of the Cloth Halls in exemplary manner. Within the Cloth Halls, the large hall, which is decorated with the town coat of arms and symbols of the guilds, contains wooden stalls selling mementos and art objects.

The Juliusz Słowacki Theatre.

The chambers in the upper floor of the Cloth Halls house the Gallery of Nineteenth-Century Polish Painting. At present it is a section of the **National Museum**, whose foundation is connected with the Cloth Halls. It was here, on this very spot, that the National Museum was opened in Cracow in the year 1883. The collection began with a gift by Henryk Siemiradzki, who donated his painting »Nero's Torches« in 1879, thereby marking the beginning of the creation of a national art collection. Paintings by, amongst others, Jan Matejko, Piotr Michałowski, Henryk Siemiradzki, Józef Chełmoński, Henryk Rodakowski and the Gierymski brothers, as well as sculptures by Pius Weloński and Walery Gadomski were gathered here. It should be mentioned at this point that the collection of Polish Art of the Twentieth Century is located in the so-called »new building« at 1, Avenue of May 3. The priceless collection of guild craft, stretching from the Middle Ages to the Twentieth Century, can be seen in the Szołayski House at 9, Szczepański Square.

On the east side of the market square stands the **Adam Mickiewicz Monument**, which was created by Teodor Rygier in 1898. After being destroyed in 1940, it was reconstructed in 1955 and re-erected on its former site. The little Romanesque *św. Wojciecha*/St Adalbert's Church near the Mickiewicz Monument is also of interest. The origins of the church reach back to the end of the tenth

»Lady with Ermine«, painting by Leonardo da Vinci.

century, but it was often changed structurally. From Grodzka Street you can see the Romanesque portal from the beginning of the twelfth century an the 17th-century dome.

On our walk we now come to the **Church of Our Lady**, Cracow's main church. It is a monument to the honour and the fame of the citizens of Cracow. The beginnings of the church date back to the first years of the thirteenth century. Its present appearance is a result of rebuilding work in the fourteenth century. The splendid Gothic choir was built in the middle of the fourteenth century, the triple-aisled nave at the end of the fourteenth century. In the first half of the fifteenth century side chapels were added. Two towers of differing height stand on the west side. The higher

Interior of the Church of the Holy Cross.

one (81 m) still has its original late-Gothic helm roof, which is topped by a spire with a Baroque crown. For centuries the tower served as the town's watchtower. This is the reason why the reveille (*Hejnal*) with its fascinating, abruptly interrupted melody sounds from its windows every hour. This is the musical symbol of Cracow. The reason why the melody of the *Hejnal* breaks off is that it recalls the sudden death of the sentry who was allegedly hit by a Tartar arrow just as he was sounding the alarm.

The Church of Our Lady is a triple-aisled basilica with a splendid elongated choir, which is surrounded by buttresses crowned with little decorative turrets. Beside the main entrance, a plaque affixed to the wall of the side chapel commemorates the bicentennial of the relief of Vienna. It was created by the sculptor Pius Weloński. Through the late-Baroque vestibule you walk past the early-Gothic holy-water font and enter the extensive church. Beneath the choir gallery you will see impressive pews, on the left side the sixteenth-century seating for the councillors and on the right side the seventeenth-century jury benches. The visitor is captivated by the beautiful wall paintings, created by Jan Matejko at the end of the last century. Passing the Baroque altars, which stand at the pillars, you approach the choir, which contains the Veit Stoß altar created by this master craftsman and his assistants in the years 1477 to 1489. On the altar shrine of the pentaptych the artist has portrayed the Death of Mary and the Assumption. On the side wings you can find scenes from the lives of Christ and Mary. On the crest you can see the Coronation of Mary surrounded by the figures of the patrons of Poland, St Stanislas and St Adalbert. This masterpiece by Veit Stoß is the most important example of late-medieval sculpture. Behind the altar you can see the priceless medieval stained-glass windows dating from the end of the fourteenth century.

The seating in the choir is an outstanding example of Cracow carving work from the first half of the seventeenth century. At the triumphal arch you can see the two monumental tombs of the patrician families Montelupi (on the left) and Cellari (at the entrance to the sacristy), dating from the early seventeenth century. The stone cross in the south aisle is a further work by Veit Stoß worth looking at. It stands close to an exquisite alabaster ciborium which was created in the second half of the sixteenth century by the Italian artist Gian Maria Padovano. Opposite the ciborium, at the triumphal arch, you will find a Baroque altar with a depiction of the Annunciation, painted by the famous Venetian artist Giambattista Pittoni in the first half of the eighteenth century. The Boner Chapel in the north aisle with its marvellous examples of Nuremberg casting work – the memorial slab to the royal dignitary Seweryn Boner and his wife Zofia née Betman from the workshop of Hans Vischer, dating from the first half of the sixteenth century – is also worth a visit.

When leaving the Church of Our Lady you step out onto the picturesque square in front of the church. Here stands the little Gothic **St Barbara's Church**. On entering it you pass a late-Gothic sculpture depicting »Christ on the Mount of Olives« with sculptures of artists from Veit Stoß circle. In the late-Baroque interior a pietà dating from the beginning of the fifteenth century stands next to the high altar.

A copy of Veit Stoß's sculpture »Christ on the Mount of Olives« has been let into the wall at the house No. 8, on the level of the first storey. The original is kept in the National Museum.

Our walk leads us back to the market square, from where we will stroll through the so-called »A-B line« and take a look at the **houses around the market square**. Memorial plaques commemorate the visits of Tadeusz Kościuszko (45 Market Square) and of Goethe (36 Market Square). The Krzysztofory Palace (No. 35)

44

Salon in the Jan Matejko House.

was originally built in the Middle Ages, but its present appearance dates from the second half of the seventeenth century. Nowadays it houses the Museum of the History of Cracow. On the first floor you can see stucco work by the Italian sculptor Baldassare Fontana, dating from the end of the seventeenth century. Next to the Krzysztofory Palace stands the splendid Spiski Palace (No. 34). In its present appearance the Palace »To the Rams« (No. 27) dates from the second half of the nineteenth century. Since 1956 its vaulted cellar has housed the political cabaret »Cellar of the Rams«, which still enriches Cracow's cultural life.

Opposite the Palace »To the Rams« there stands the Town Hall Tower, a remnant of the former town hall that was torn down at the beginning of the last century. Today the tower contains a section of the Museum of History. A plaque let into the ground next to the tower bears as an inscription the oath taken by Tadeusz Kościuszko here on 24 March 1794. From the Palace »To the Rams« we come to *Ulica św. Anny*/St Anne's Street, and continue on it in the direction of the Collegium Maius and the St Anne's Church. At No. 6 you will find the imposing classical building of the former Collegium Physicum, which dates from the end of the eighteenth century (now the Kołłątaj Collegium). A memorial plaque on its facade commemorates the achievement of two professors of the

Jagiellonian University, Karol Olszewski and Zygmund Wrób-lewski, who were the first to condense oxygen and nitrogen out of the air (1883). At the corner of St Anne's Street and *Ulica Jagiellońska*/Jagiellon Street you can see the Gothic building of the **Collegium Maius**–the oldest preserved university building, dating back to the early fifteenth century. The entrance to the Collegium Maius is located on Jagiellon Street, right next to a striking Gothic oriel protruding from the facade of the building. The complex of the Collegium Maius, whose four wings enclose an arcaded courtyard, was built towards the end of the fifteenth century together with its former buildings, and was intended as living space for the professors as well as for lectures. The lecture rooms were situated on the ground floor, the upper storey contained the living quarters of the professors, the theology lecture hall as well as a communal dining room, the so-called *Stuba communis*. At the beginning of the fifteenth century the library (*Libraria*) was added. Since the renovation of the Collegium Maius after World War II the Museum of the Jagiellonian University has been located here. It contains memorabilia of professors, the university treasure (including the vice-chancellor's sceptre and the famous Jagiellonian globe with a depiction of America) as well as valuable scientific apparatus. Furthermore, the museum owns an interesting gallery of portraits of former university professors.

From the corner of Jagiellon and St Anne's Street you can see the **Collegiate Church of St Anne**. The most splendid Baroque church in Cracow was built between 1689 and 1703 on the site of an earlier Gothic church which had also been a university church. The church was designed by Tylman van Gameren, who used the most important Roman buildings of the time as models, i.e. the works of Carlo Maderna and Giovanni Lorenzo Bernini. Most of the spacious interior is adorned with remarkable sculptural stucco decoration, which was carried out by Baldassare Fontana. The paintings in the nave and the chancel are the work of Karl Dankwart; the dome was painted by Carlo and Innocenzo Monti. The high altar contains a painting of St Anne by Jerzy Eleuter Siemiginowski; the late-Baroque paintings near the choir stalls are by Szymon Czechowicz. The transept contains the altar grave of St Jan Kanty/Johannes Cantius, who was professor of theology at the Cracow Academy. Opposite the grave, in the west arm of the transept, there stands an altar with a magnificently designed stucco relief of the pietà. Next to it you can see a monument of Mikołaj Kopernik/Nicolaus Copernicus, designed by Sebastian Sierakowski

Adam Mickiewicz Monument on the market square.

Altar by Veit Stoß in the Church of Our Lady.

at the beginning of the nineteenth century – a homage by the university to Copernicus, the greatest luminary of the Cracow Academy. The picturesque and elegant interior of the Collegiate Church of St Anne is one of the major achievements of the Polish Baroque age and is a particularly good example of the influence of Roman Baroque art, especially through the work of Giovanni Lorenzo Bernini.

Opposite the St Anne's Church stands the seventeenth-century building of the Nowodworski Collegium, which was formerly the oldest grammar school in Poland and enjoyed the patronage of the Cracow Academy from 1588 on. The arcaded courtyard is worth visiting. You should take the time to walk down the *Planty* to the left, to the Collegium Novum (1883–1887). It was erected by the architect Feliks Księżarski and houses the office of the vice-chancellor of the Jagiellonian University as well as the dean's offices. Between the Collegium Novum and the old Collegium Physicum (beginning of the 20th c.) you can see a monument of Mikołaj Kopernik/Nicolaus Copernicus by Cyprian Godebski, placed in the middle of a green space. It was donated in 1900 on the occasion of the 500th anniversary of the renewal of the university through Władysław Jagiełło. Our route now leads back to the market square and then on in the direction of Grodzka Street. On the market square at the corner of Bracka Street there stands the

The Church of Our Lady.

Tombstone of Callimachus by Veit Stoß, in the Dominican Church.

Zbaraski Palace (No. 20), which possesses a classical facade from the second half of the eighteenth century and an arcaded courtyard from the first half of the seventeenth century. The Hetmans House at No. 17 has a lovely Gothic hall on the ground floor, which is adorned with keystones decorated in relief dating from the second half of the fourteenth century. Opposite the little St Adalbert's Church lies the world-famous *Wierzynek* restaurant (16 Market Square). According to tradition, councillor Mikołaj Wierzynek wined and dined the participants of a gathering of kings here in the

The Town Hall Tower.

year 1364. Among the guests who had come to Cracow on the invitation of Casimir the Great were Emperor Charles IV and King Ludwig of Hungary. Wierzynek's banquet became legendary.

Along **Grodzka Street** we come to *Plac Dominikański/*Dominican Square, where the Gothic ***Kościół św. Trojcy z klasztorem ojców dominikanow*/Dominican Church of the Holy Trinity** and the Dominican monastery stand. The Dominicans came to Cracow in 1222. The church was rebuilt several times, and received its final appearance of a triple-aisled basilica in the fifteenth century.

Frequent fires diminished the splendour of the church. One of the worst fires occurred in 1850, when the old interior furnishings were destroyed and the church partly became a ruin. A lovely Gothic portal leads into the neo-Gothic interior of the church, which dates from after the fire storm of 1850. Located on the left side of the chancel is the bronze epitaph to the Italian humanist Fillipo Buonaccorsi (Callimachus; died 1496) who was tutor to the sons of Kazimierz Jagiellończyk. The epitaph, designed by Veit Stoß, was cast in the Nuremberg workshop of Peter Vischer the Elder. Nearby, on the same wall, you will find the memorial slab of the Cracow Duke Leszek Czarny/Leszek the Black (died 1288), to whose consent the town owed the erection of a stone defence system. The nave is surrounded by chapels, of which the Renaissance Chapel of św. Jacek/St Hyacinth in the upper storey, with paintings by Tomaso Dolabella and stucco work by Baldassare Fontana, deserves particular mention. At the entrance to the chapel you can see two large paintings by Dolabella: The Wedding of Canaan and The Last Supper (first half of the 17th c.). Opposite the Chapel of St Hyacinth lies the mannerist Myszkowski Chapel, which was erected at the beginning of the seventeenth century. It is famous for its unique gallery of 16 high relief busts of members of the Myszkowski family in the lower part of the dome. Two interesting chapels are situated next to the church exit, to the right the Zbaraski Chapel (second quarter of the 17th c.) with an elliptical dome and the tombs of Princes Jerzy and Krzysztof Zbaraski, and to the left the early-Baroque Chapel of the Princes Lubomirski. To the north, Gothic cloisters adjoin the church, replete with tombs, epitaphs and memorial slabs. There you can also find late-Romanesque wall fragments of the older church as well as the brick chapter hall from the middle of the thirteenth century.

Situated opposite, already on *Plac Wszystkich Świętych*/All Saints Square, are the ***Kościół i Klasztor ojców franciszkanow*/Franciscan Church** and Monastery from the thirteenth century. One of its founders was Prince Bolesław Wstydliwy/Boleslav the Chaste (died 1279). The church was destroyed in the fire of 1850. After its restoration it was fitted out in neo-Gothic style, including the altars and pews. The painting of the chancel and the transept as well as the magnificent stained-glass windows in the chancel are the work of Stanisław Wyspiański. This important artist also created the expressive glass window »God the Father« in the west window of the nave. Without doubt this composition is the most beautiful example of stained-glass art from the beginning of our

»God the Father« window by St. Wyspiański, Franciscan Church.

century. The nave was painted by Tadeusz Popiel. In the transept, immediately next to the side entrance, hangs a painting depicting the Blessed Salomea, the sister of Bolesław Wstydliwy/Boleslav the Chaste, whose mortal remains rest in a niche above the altar, protected by a grille. To the north, the nave is joined by a side aisle (today the Chapel of the Sufferings of Christ) with Stations of the Cross painted by Józef Mehoffer. Located opposite, on the south side, is the Mater Dolorosa Chapel with a late-Gothic painting of the Mother of Sorrows. This chapel leads to the cloister of the monastery (a second entrance to the cloister is to be found in the transept). There you can see a unique collection of portraits of Cracow bishops, which gives a good impression of sixteenth-century Polish portrait painting. The walls of the cloister are covered with Gothic wall paintings from the middle of the fifteenth century. A fine painting of the Annunciation and depictions of the stigmatisation of St Francis and of Christ being tortured in a winepress are particularly worth mentioning.

After leaving the church through the west portal you will see the monument of Cardinal Adam Stefan Sapieha (died 1951), the work of sculptor August Zamoyski.

Opposite the Franciscan Church, on *Ulica Franciszkańska/* Franciscan Street lies the **Bishop's Palace**, whose present appearance dates from the seventeenth century, though its original buildings go back to the fourteenth century. Cardinal Karol Wojtyła, now Pope John Paul II, lived in this palace from 1964 to 1978. A monument to Pope John Paul II by Jole Sensi Croci stands in the inner courtyard.

Our walk now leads us back to Grodzka Street. Next to the Franciscan Church you can see the monument to Dr Józef Dietl (died 1878), vice-chancellor of the Jagiellonian University and the first mayor of Cracow. It was created by Xawery Dunikowski, the most well-known twentieth-century Polish sculptor. Visible behind the monument is the massive building of the Wielopolski Palace, now the seat of the Cracow town council. On a green area there stands the small monument to Mikołaj Zyblikiewicz (died 1887), the second mayor of Cracow, who rendered outstanding services to Cracow and Galicia during the period of the town's autonomy. The sculpture is the work of Walery Gadomski.

From here our walk takes us along Grodzka Street in the direction of the Wawel. A memorial plaque on the corner of Grodzka and Poselska Street (39–41 Grodzka Street) calls attention to the fact that Veit Stoß once lived here. A little further, on the left hand side stands the ***Kościół św. św. Piotra i Pawła/***

Jagiellonian University, Collegium Maius.

Church of Sts Peter and Paul, which was founded by King
Zygmunt III Waza/Sigismund III Wasa for the Jesuits and was
built between 1597 and 1630. The church is the earliest example of early Baroque architecture in Cracow; the plans of the
church were sent by Giovanni de Rosis from Rome. The building was completed by Giovanni Trevano, who in the end, created a church modelled on the *Il Gesù* in Rome (this work has
been lately attributed to M. Castello). The square in front of the
church is separated from the street by a small enclosed space
with stone figures of the tvelves apostles (now free copies of the
18th-c. figures by David Hül). The spacious interior with its
side chapels and transept is adorned with rich stucco decoration,

55

especially in the apse (the work of Giovanni Battista Falconi from the first half of the 17th century). The high altar contains a painting by Józef Brodowski from the first half of the seventeenth century, depicting the handing over of the key. Located on the left hand side is the splendid Baroque tomb of Cracow bishop Andrzej Trzebicki, who died in the year 1679. The famous preacher Piotr Skarga, who died in the year 1612, is buried in the crypt below the chancel; his marble memorial slab, created by Oskar Sosnowski, adorns the nave. The church also contains various beautiful classical monuments from the nineteenth century, as well as sculptures from the early twentieth century. The *Ecce Homo* by Marcelo Guyski, the monument to Maurycy Poniatowski by Wiktor Brodzki and the statue of Maurycy Drużbacki by Antoni Madeyski are also worth mentioning. In the nave you will find the monument of Kajetan Florkiewicz, the work of Franciszek Wyspiański, and a monument of Pope Pius IX by Walery Gadomski and Michał Korpal stands against one of the dome pillars.

On leaving the Church of Sts Peter and Paul you look towards the building of the former Collegium Iuridicum (53 Grodzka Street), complete with a splendid Baroque portal and an arcaded courtyard from the first half of the seventeenth century.

The Romanesque twin-towered **Kościół św. Andrzeja/St Andrew's Church** is certainly worth a visit. Founded at the end of the eleventh century, it was built in the course of the twelfth century as the main church of Okół, a settlement outside the town. During the Tartar invasion in the year 1241 the church withstood the invaders and offered the people protection within its walls, as is reported by the historiographer Jan Długosz. In the early fourteenth century the St Clare Sisters moved here and took the church into their care. The interior was completely redone in Baroque style in the late seventeenth century. The exceptional stucco work is presumed to be the work of Baldassare Fontana from the first years of the eighteenth century, whereas the paintings were created by Karl Dankwart.

Situated on Grodzka Street, right behind the St Clare Convent, is the early-Baroque *Kościół św. Marcina*/St Martin's Church with a simple facade, presumably the work of Trevano. Since the beginning of the nineteenth century this church has belonged to the Cracow community of the Protestant Augsburg Confession. The interior contains a crucifix dating from the fourteenth century and an altar painting by Henryk Siemiradzki depicting Christ calming the storm.

Bishop's Palace.

Continuing on from Grodzka Street to Senacka Street, we come to the *Ulica Kanonicza*/**Kanonicza Street**. Here the canons of the Cracow cathedral chapter built their residences. Almost all the houses bear interesting architectural details, and the whole street has a special atmosphere. The biographical **Stanisław Wyspiański Museum** is located at No. 9. Now in close proximity to the Wawel, the two Renaissance courtyards of house No. 18 are worth visiting (the work of Jan Michałowicz from Urzędów) as is the former residence of the cathedral chapter deans, the so-called deanery house at No. 21, the rebuilding of which was partly carried out by the Italian architect and sculptor Santi Gucci. At No. 19 there is located Archidiecesan Museum. The **Jan Długosz House** (No. 25) is where the great historian and tutor to the sons of Kazimierz Jagiellończyk worked. In the 19th century this house contained the sculpture workshop of Franciszek Wyspiański, the father of Stanisław Wyspiański who spent his childhood here. Affixed to the side facing the Wawel are plagues – a late-Gothic plague recalling the foundation of the house of the psalmists by Długosz and a modern plague dedicated to Stanislaw Wyspiański, the work of Bronisław Chromy. Affixed to this house is also a Baroque picture of the Virgin Mary with the Child Jesus, which, according to legend, was riddled by bullets during one the Swedish attacks.

57

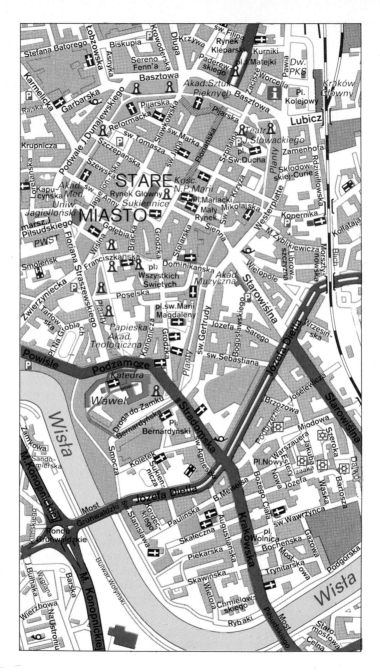

Wawel Hill

Ulica Kanonicza/Kanonicza Street • Tadeusz Kaściuszko Monument • Brama Herbowa/Coat of Arms Gate Brama Wazów/Wasa Gate • Cathedral • Royal Graves Cathedral Museum • Royal Palace • Exhibition »Wawel Zaginiony«/»The Lost Wawel« Smocza Jama/Dragon's Cave

Two approaches lead onto the Wawel, the one from the direction of Bernardyńska Street and the other from **Kanonicza Street**, which is the historical access road. In the vicinity of the deanery you already have a good view of the north wing of the Royal Palace, with the tower of Sigismund III on the left side and the so-called Sobieski Tower on the right. Furthermore, you can see the Cathedral with the treasure house and the Sigismund Tower as well as the even taller Clock Tower. The steep road is flanked by a wall covered with so-called Wawel bricks, into which have been chiselled the names of institutions and individuals whose contributions helped restore the Wawel during the wars. On a bastion in the distance you can see the 16th-century **Tadeusz Kościuszko Monument**, which was set up here in 1921. It was cast to a design by Leonardo Marconi, a sculptor from Lwow. Having been destroyed in World War II, the monument was re-erected in 1960 as a gift from the town of Dresden.

Passing through the ***Brama Herbowa*/Coat of Arms Gate**, which is decorated with the coats of arms of those territories that used to belong to the republic of the two nations (Poland and the former Lithuania), and then through the Baroque ***Brama Wazów*/ Wasa Gate** you come to the courtyard of the Cathedral. Here our sightseeing tour begins. The **Cathedral** on the Wawel is one of the most venerable churches in Poland. It is a memorial of artistic and patriotic character and has been a monument of the history of the Polish people and of the fame of Poland since the nineteenth century. The first cathedral located on this site was built in the year 1000. It was founded by Bolesław Chroby/Boleslav the Brave. The building of the so-called Second Wawel Cathedral is thought to have been begun by Duke Władysław Herman, and it was later

The route of the walk is marked in grey in the map opposite.

finished by Bolesław Krzywousty/Boleslav Squintmouth. This cathedral remained standing until the year 1305, when it was destroyed in a fire. The Gothic Cathedral, in which the coronations and the burials of kings took place, was built at the instigation of the Cracow Bishop Nanker and King Władysław Łokiełek/ Ladislav the Short.

The building work, which began in the year 1320, was not completed until 1364. With only few exceptions, all Polish kings were crowned and buried on the Wawel from the time of Ladislav the Short onwards. Beginning in the nineteenth century, national heroes and poets were also laid to rest in the subterranean vaults of the Cathedral. The great task of restoring the cathedral building, which had begun to deteriorate, was started at the turn of the nineteenth century. The restoration work was overseen by the excellent architects Sławomir Odrzywolski and Zygmunt Hendel, and the Cathedral has remained unchanged since then.

The Gothic cathedral building is surrounded by chapels dating from various periods, amongst which the *Kaplica Zygmuntowska*/ Sigismund Chapel with its golden dome should receive particular mention. The Cathedral is framed by three towers, of which the oldest is the *Wieża Wikaryjska*/Vicar's Tower, also known as *Wieża Srebrnych Dzwonów*/Silver Bells Tower. To the north stand the *Wieża Zegarowa*/Clock Tower with a Baroque roof dating from the early eighteenth century, and the slightly lower *Wieża Zygmuntowska*/Sigismund Tower. The latter is known for the so-called Sigismund bell, which was cast by Hans Beham in 1520 for King Zygmunt I Stary/Sigismund I the Old. The bell is only rung on the highest Church feast days and on the occasion of national ceremonies. The Cathedral is surrounded by a Baroque wall with three small gates. You enter the church through a metal-covered portal which recalls the time of Casimir the Great, his initial (K) being repeated many times on the door. Animal bones from the glacial period hang on chains above the entrance door-formerly they were credited with having magical powers for banishing evil. In its present form the Cracow Cathedral is a triple-aisled basilica with a transept and an ambulatory, with a wreath of chapels surrounding the entire building. Located in the centre of the cathedral is the Baroque mausoleum (1626–1629) of St Stanislaw, the work of Giovanni Trevano (it has been lately attributed to M. Castello). It costains the silver sarcophagus with the relict of St Stanislas, the former bishop of Cracow and the patron of Poland, which was created in the Danzig workshop of Peter von der Rennen in teh second half of the 17th century.

Royal Cathedral on the Wawel.

Before the mausoleum stands the sarcophagus of King Władysław Jagiełło, the victor of Grunwald, complete with a Renaissance canopy. To the left you will find the symbolic sarcophagus of King Władysław Warneńczyk, created in the early twentieth century by Antoni Madeyski. Above the royal tombs, the walls of the nave are hung with splendid seventeenth-century tapestries depicting the biblical story of Jacob. They were woven in Brussels and were a gift from Bishop Jan Małachowski.

Located behind the mausoleum is the chancel with choir stalls from the early seventeenth century and the Baroque high altar

61

Sarcophagus of St Stanislas.

(mid-17th c.), in front of which the coronations took place. The painting of Christ is ascribed to Marcin Blechowski. On the left side of the altar there stands a monument to Cardinal Adam Stefan Sapieha (died 1951), created by Jadwiga Horodyska. The memorial slab of Cardinal Fryderyk Jagiellończyk at the foot of the altar is also worth noting. It was cast in the Vischer workshop in the early sixteenth century.

From the chancel we now proceed to the north aisle. Passing the Gothic sarcophagus of King Władysław Łokiełek/Ladislav the Short you come to the sacristy, from which stairs lead into the Sigismund Tower, where you can see the Sigismund bell. From here we return to the north aisle to look at the graves of Adam

Part of the tomb of King Ladislav the Short.

Mickiewicz and Juliusz Słowacki. Mickiewicz was interred on the Wawel in 1890, Juliusz Słowacki in the year 1927. Opposite the crypt in which both poets rest you can see a silver relief in a stone frame. It depicts King Jan III Sobieski near Vienna and was created by Józef Hakowski as a copy of the well-known painting by Jan Matejko, which is part of the Vatican collections. Adjacent to the sacristy lies the Zebrzydowski Chapel, in which the sixteenth-century tomb of Bishop Andrzej Zebrzydowski is worth noticing. It was created by the important Polish sculptor Jan Michałowicz from Urzędów, who was later called the »Polish Praxiteles«.

Past the sarcophagus of Władysław Łokiełek we now enter the eastern section of the ambulatory. In a late-Baroque altar on the north side you will find the famous black crucifix, before which Queen Jadwiga/Hedwig is said to have prayed. The altar has contained her relics since 1987; they were brought to the altar by Pope John Paul II. This section of the ambulatory contains the tombs of King Michał Korybut Wiśniowiecki and King Jan III Sobieski as well as those of their queens Eleonore of Habsburg and Maria Kazimiera. They were designed in the mid-eighteenth century by the famous Italian architect Francesco Placidi. Opposite lies the Chapel of St Stefan Batory. The tomb was created by Santi Gucci at the behest of Queen Anna Jagiellonka. The Batory Chapel, also known as the Chapel of Our Lady, is flanked by the Chapel of Bishop Piotr Tomicki on the right and by the Chapel of Bishop Piotr Gamrat on the left. The tombs of these ecclesiastical dignitaries were created by Gian Maria Padovano.

The most striking feature of the south section of the ambulatory is the Gothic sarcophagus of King Casimir the Great, the founder of the Cracow Academy. It is assumed that the sarcophagus was commissioned by Elżbieta Łokietkówna, Casimir's sister, and her son, King Ludwig of Hungary. Opposite lies the Chapel of King Jan Olbracht/John Albert. The king's late-Gothic tomb is situated in an arcade of double pilasters and was made by Francesco Fiorentino in the early sixteenth century. This sepulchre was donated by Jan Olbracht's mother, Queen Elisabeth of Habsburg, together with the then royal prince and later king Zygmunt I Stary/Sigismund the Old. Walking further through the ambulatory you pass two Baroque chapels, the Zadzik Chapel and the Konarski Chapel. The altar in the Chapel of Bishop Jakub Zadzik contains a depiction of John the Baptist, painted by Wojciech Korneli Stattler in the first half of the nineteenth century using a portrait of Adam Mickiewiczs as John the Baptist. Exhibited in a glass case in front of the Chapel of Bishop Jan Konarski are fragments of the sceptre and orb that were taken from the grave of Queen Jadwiga in the year 1949. Adjacent lies the sarcophagus of Queen Jadwiga, which was sculpted by Antono Madeyski out of Carrara marble in the early twentieth century. The queen's mortal remains, which had previously been buried before the high altar, rested here from 1949 to 1987.

Located opposite the sarcophagus of Queen Jadwiga is the famous *Kaplica Zygmuntowska*/Sigismund Chapel, which is referred to as »the pearl of the Renaissance north of the Alps«. It is the most important Renaissance work of art in Poland, and almost became the symbol of the »Golden Age«. It was donated by King Zygmunt I Stary/Sigismund I the Old, and was built to the design

The »Zygmunt/Sigismund« Bell.

of the Florentine architect Bartolomeo Berrecci between 1519 and
1531. Almost the entire interior of the chapel is covered with
grotesquerie, presumably the work of Giovanni Cini from Siena.
The mausoleum of the last Jagiellons, the kings Zygmunt I
Stary/Sigismund I the Old and Zygmunt August/Sigismund
Augustus, is situated on the right; in the centre is the entrance to
the tomb of Queen Anna Jagiellonka. Both the tombs of Sigismund

Sarcophagus of King Casimir the Great.

Augustus and of Anna Jagiellonka were created by Santi Gucci, the tomb of Sigismund I the Old by Berecci. The altar, a wonderful example of both the goldsmith's art and painting, is the joint work of the Nuremberg craftsmen Peter Flötner, Melchior Baier and Georg Pencz. The chapel is crowned by a dome, the interior of which is decorated with stone rosettas in coffers. The grating that closes off the chapel was cast in the workshop of Hans Vischer in Nuremberg. Portraits of King Sigismund I the Old and of Anna Jagiellonka hang above the entrance to the chapel.

After leaving the ambulatory you enter the south aisle. Located opposite the sarcophagus of Władysław Jagiełło is the Baroque Wasa Chapel, which was built by King Jan Kazimierz/John

Romanesque St Leonard Crypt with royal graves.

Casimir in the second half of the seventeenth century. It is closed off by a bronze grating which was cast in Danzig by Michael Weinhold in the year 1673. The last chapel in this row is the Chapel of the Potocki Family, which contains a sculpture of Jesus giving his blessing, created by the famous Danish classical sculptor Bertel Thorvaldsen. The altar contains a painting by Guercino da Cento which depicts the Crucifixion (17th c.). On the right stands the mannerist tomb of Bishop Filip Padniewski (died 1572), the work of the Polish sculptor Jan Michałowicz.

Affixed to the wall to the left of the Potocki Chapel is a bronze plaque portraying Piotr Kmita. Dating from the early sixteenth century, it was cast in the workshop of Peter Vischer.

Interior of the Sigismund Chapel with tombs.

From the north, the south aisle is completed by the Chapel of the Holy Cross, which King Kazimierz Jagiellończyk and his wife Elisabeth of Habsburg had erected in the second half of the fifteenth century. The walls of the chapel and the Gothic vaulted ceiling are covered with Russian-Byzantine paintings, which were executed by painters from Pskow. In the corner of the chapel there stands the sarcophagus of King Kazimierz Jagiellończyk (died 1492). It was created by Veit Stoß, merely the capitals of the columns supporting the canopy being by Jörg Huber from Passau. The chapel also contains two Gothic tryptychs: the Holy Trinity tryptych (1467) and the tryptych of the Mother of Sorrows (late-15th c.). Unfortunately, the size of the tomb of Bishop Kajetan

Tomb of King Kazimierz Jagiellończyk by Veit Stoß.

Sołtyk, which was included here in the late eighteenth century, somewhat spoils the harmony of the predominantly Gothic interior. The glass windows were designed by Józef Mehoffer.

In the nave we turn to the Czartoryski Chapel, which is situated in the Clock Tower. To the left, the north aisle is completed by the Chapel of the Holy Trinity, which was decorated with patriotic wall paintings by Włodzmierz Tetmajer at the beginning of the twentieth century. A statue of Włodzimierz Potocki, who died in the year 1812, sculpted by Bertel Thorvaldsen, stands at the entrance to the chapel.

From the Czartoryski Chapel, which contains a tryptych from the sixteenth century, we descend to the **royal graves**. It was only from the mid-sixteenth century on that the Polish kings were laid to rest in the crypts beneath Wawel Cathedral. The first to be buried here was King Zygmunt I Stara/Sigismund I the Old. His predecessors lie in burial vaults beneath the cathedral floor. Apart from kings, national heroes such as Tadeusz Kościuszko, Prince Józef Poniatowski and Field Marshal Józef Piłsudski were also laid to rest in the subterranean vaults of the cathedral. The royal burial place begins with the Romanesque Crypt of St Leonard, a relict of the so-called Herman's Cathedral.

Orientation notices on the walls help guide the visitor through the Wawel necropolises. The metal coffins made in Danzig in the 16th and 17teenth centuries deserve particular mention, as do the fine coffins of Ladislav IV Wasa and Cäcilia Renata, which were made by goldsmith Johann Christian Bierpfaff in Thorn. The royal graves are ended by the Crypt of Field Marshal Józef Piłsudski, which lies in front of the Crypt of the Wasa Dynasty.

Since 1978 the chapter houses in front of the Cathedral have housed the **Cathedral Museum**. Exhibited here are choice items from the cathedral treasure and the chapter archives as well as from the chapter library. In addition to liturgical objects you will find burial crowns and devotional objects of kings, bishops and national heroes on display. Special exhibition cases contain simple mementos of the former Archbishop of Cracow Karol Wojtyła, now Pope John Paul II.

From the Cathedral Museum on the south side our walk takes us to the Royal Palace, the former residence of the Piast, Jagiellon and Wasa families, a centre of cultural, political and artistic life. The original building on the site was a Romanesque palace, which was followed in the 14th century by a Gothic castle, and, finally, in the 16th century by the Renaissance palace, which King Sigismund I the Old had built by the architects Eberhard von Koblenz, Francesco Fiorentino, Benedykt of Sandomierz and Bartolomeo Berrecci. The palace has a rectangular courtyard lined with arcaded passages. In former times the Renaissance architecture was complemented by art collections which endowed the interiors of the spacious apartments with additional splendour. The rooms are decorated with coffered ceilings and friezes below the ceilings. The most precious ornamentation of the rooms, however, was a unique collection of tapestries owned by Sigismund Augustus. The monarch had commissioned them from the best weavers in Brussels. Amongst the designers of the tapestries particular mention should be made of Michiel Coxcie. In his will, Sigismund Augustus bequeathed this impressive collection of approx. 350

Senators' Hall with Sigismund Augustus's tapestries.

pieces to the Polish state, thereby setting a precedent. After much confusion during the course of the centuries, 142 of these tapestries now hang in Wawel Palace once more. They are exhibited in the rooms on the second floor. The painted friezes below the ceilings in the halls on the second floor, which were executed by Antoni from Breslau and Hans Dürer, also date from the time of Sigismund Augustus. The Envoy's Hall, which is also known as the »Hall Beneath the Heads«, is unique in Europe. Some of the carvings of human heads from the original coffered ceiling have been preserved, and in fact the coffered ceiling has also been reconstructed. In the year 1595 two fires devastated parts of the palace. The north wing burnt down almost entirely, and was later rebuilt in Baroque style by Giovanni Battista Trevano, who also designed the monumental staircase.

The Wawel's days of splendour finally came to an end in the memorable year of 1609, when Sigismund III left Cracow and marched against Moscow. He never returned to Cracow but established his seat in Warsaw. From this time on the rooms of Wawel Palace were only used on occasions such as coronations or funerals–the palace fell into disrepair. In 1655 the Swedes sacked the Wawel, and in 1702 a large fire devastated the palace. The former splendour of the royal seat of the Jagiellons and the Wasa had been destroyed, and there followed the period of national bondage. The royal apartments were occupied by the Austrians, the army setting up barracks here. It was not until 1880 that Emperor Franz Joseph I gave his permission that the Polish people could buy the royal palace back from the army. After this had been successfully achieved in the early twentieth century, work on an extensive restoration of the building began under the direction of the architects Hendel and Szyszko-Bohusz, through which the palace regained its splendid appearance.

After Poland had received its independence in the year 1918, efforts to bring back the original furnishings of the interior were begun. After the treaty of Riga, Russia gave back many works of art, amongst them the tapestries and the coronation sword »*Szczerbiec*«. Renaissance and Baroque furniture and paintings, either bequeathed or bought, returned some of the palace's former splendour. Unfortunately, there was not much time to enjoy the result of the conservation work, as the years of Hitler's rule were to follow. The Germans turned the palace into the headquarters of the general governor Hans Frank. This sombre time for the Wawel and the Poles lasted until 1945. After the war, the Wawel treasure, including the *Szczerbiec* and the tapestries, returned in two instalments (1959 and 1961) from Canada, to where it had been evacuated out of fear of the Germans. The royal palace, the former royal seat, once more became the most magnificent Polish museum, in which valuable works of art are exhibited. In addition to the palace rooms, mention should also be made of the royal treasure chamber, the armoury and the impressive exhibition »The East in the Wawel Collections«, which contains oriental objects. In order to view this exhibition you need special permission from the palace administration. The royal treasure chamber, the armoury and the palace rooms, on the other hand, are open to visitors. As the exhibits of the royal treasure chamber and the armoury are all provided with information labels, they need not be discussed here and can be viewed on one's own. The palace rooms, however, can only be viewed with a guide, who explains the furnishings of the indvidual rooms and their priceless works of art in detail.

A further museum is also situated on the Wawel, an archaeological museum which shows excavation work as well as models of the buildings that used to stand on the Wawel. The exhibition »*Wawel Zaginiony*«/»**The Lost Wawel**« contains the early medieval rotunda of the Chapel of Our Lady, which was erected in the second half of the tenth century. Round about the rotunda you can see the different archaeological layers that

Tomb of King Kazimierz Jagiellończyk by Veit Stoß.

illustrate the history of settlement of the Wawel. The exhibition is completed by the Wawel capidarium as well as by a collection of Renaissance and Baroque tiles together with an interesting display of old stoves which have been carefully reconstructed.

On the square in front of the Cathedral you will see the foundations of two mediewal churches, St Michael's Church and St George's Church; to the south stand reconstructed medieval defence walls. On the left you can see the Gothic Senators' Bastion, on the right the Sandomierska/Sandomierz Bastion. To the west stands the Thieves' Bastion.

If you have the time, you can visit an oddity on Wawel Hill; the *Smocza Jama*/**Dragon's Cave**, a lime-stone cave which is located beneath this part of the hill–a geological quirk. The entrance lies near the Thieves' Bastion. The legend claims that here lived a dragon who was killed by the legendary Prince Krak. A modern statue of a firebreathing dragon by Bronisław Chromy stands at the cave exit. From here you can walk along Bernardyńska Street to Stradom or descend from the Wawel, next to the Sandomierz Bastion, and walk in the same direction until you reach the Bernardine Church. From there you can view the east section of the palace in all its magnificence. Opposite to Wawel on another bank of Wisła at Konopnicka Street No 32, there is located The Centre of Japanese Fine Arts and Technics.

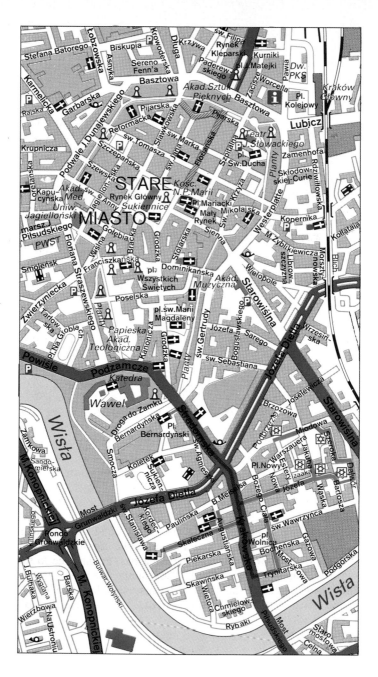

Walk
Kazimierz

Stradom • Kościół ojców bernardynów/Bernardine Church • Kościół księży misjonarzy/Missionary Church Ulica Krakowska/Krakowska Street • Kościół ojców bonifratrów/Church of the Hospitallers Wolnica Square • Ethnographical Museum Kościół Bożego Ciała/Ascension Church • Kościół ojców augustianow/Augustinian Church • Skałka z kościelem ojców paulinów/Skałka Hill with Pauline Church Polish Vault of Honour • Jewish Town • Bożnica Wysoka/High Synagogue • Bożnica Izaaka/Isaac Synagogue Bożnica Kupa/Kupa Synagogue • Ulica Szercha/Broad Street • Stara Synagoga/Old Synagogue • Bożnica Popera/ Poper Synagogue • Bożnica Remu'h/Remu'h Synagogue Cmentarz Remu'h/Remu'h Cemetery • Temple Synagogue

The village of **Stradom** has lain on the south side of the Wawel since the Middle Ages. In the early fifteenth century it was incorporated into the town of Kazimierz, which had been founded by King Kazimierz Wielki/Casimir the Great in the year 1335. Stradom was separated from Kazimierz by the river Wisła/Weichsel, which flowed along the line of the present Dietl Street. If you walk down from Wawel Hill on the southern access road, i.e. from the direction of Stradom, you will see the St Bernardine of Siena monastery complex on the right, situated on Bernardyńska Street, with the *Kościół ojców bernardynów/* **Bernardine Church**. The monks settled here in 1453; the first church was founded by Cardinal Zbigniew Oleśnicki. The present church was built after the Swedish invasion between 1670 and 1680 to a design by Krzysztof Mieroszewski. The Baroque church has a twin-towered facade and a dome at the crossing which is hidden by the roof–this for strategic reasons, mainly due to the close proximity of the Wawel. The church interior, which is fashioned in late-Baroque style, contains valuable works of art, such as altars with paintings by Franciszek Lekszycki (second half

The route of the walk is marked in grey in the map opposite.

of the 17th c.). The St Anne's Chapel to the left of the high altar contains a carved figure of St Anna Selbdritt, which is presumed to have been made in the workshop of Veit Stoß. Also noteworthy is a Dance of Death painting from the mid-seventeenth century, which was to remind people of the vanity of life and make them think about death. This painting is an interesting example from the time of the so-called sarmatism, which was later often imitated. A chapel with the relics of St Szymon from Lipnica, a Bernardine monk who died in 1482, adjoins the north side of the chancel.

After visiting the Bernardine Church, our walk leads along Stradomska Street to the Baroque *Kościół księży misjonarzy/* **Missionary Church**. It was designed in the early 18th century by the important architect Kasper Bażanka, who used works by Giovanni Lorenzo Bernini and Francesco Borromini as models. This lovely edifice possesses an unusually harmonious and homogeneous interior. The walls are decorated with mirrors which serve to enlarge the space optically. The high altar contains an 18th-century painting of the conversion of St Paul by Tadeusz Kuntze. The altar sculptures in the chapels were created in the workshop of Antoni Frączkiewicz (18th c.).

From the Missionary Church our route leads along Stradomska Street to Dietl Street, along which the Weichsel used to flow until it was filled in in the second half of the 19th century. On the right bank lay Kasimierz, which was protected by a town wall with gates. For centuries Kazimierz was an independent municipal community and as such a »satellite« of Cracow, until it was incorporated into Cracow at the end of the 18th century.

Walking along Dietl Street and into **Krakowska Street**, we come to Wolnica Square. Having crossed the square and approaching the bridge across the Weichsel, you can see the picturesque facade of the late-Baroque *Kościół ojców bonifratów/* **Church of the Hospitallers** (the former Trinitarian Church), which was designed by Francesco Placidi in the second half of the eighteenth century. Influenced by Roman buildings designed by Francesco Borromini and late-Baroque tendencies, Placidi created a single-naved church with side chapels. The result was an example of architecture of delicate lines. Depicted is St Johannes of Matha, the founder of the Trinitarian Order, with prisoners whom he has bought free from Turkish captivity.

From here we return to **Wolnica Square**, the old market square of the medieval Kazimierz. In its centre stands the old Town Hall, which was built in the 15th century. In the 16th and 17th centuries it was altered structurally, and in the second half of the 19th

Kazimierz Town Hall.

century the south side was extended. Today the former town hall houses the **Ethnographical Museum**, which was the first of its kind in Poland. The collections illustrate the life, customs and culture of the population of Cracow as well as of the inhabitants of other regions of Poland. Authentic interiors of farmhouses from the Cracow region as well as from the regions of Podhale and Silesia form an important part of the exhibition. Furthermore, the museum possesses an extensive collection of national costumes. Changing exhibitions are mounted at 46 Krakowska Street.

On the northeastern corner of Wolnica Square you can see the mighty Gothic ***Kościół Bożego Ciała*/Ascencion Church**. Founded by Casimir the Great, it was the main parish church of Kazimierz. After the edifice was completed at the beginning of the 15th century King Władysław Jagiełło summoned to Kazimierz Lateran Canons from Kłodzko/Glatz, who still look after the church today. It is one of the most impressive Gothic edifices in Cracow–a triple-aisled basilica with a mighty tower fitted with a mannerist hood (17th c.). The facade with its Gothic stepped gable with blind arcades is decorated with the coats of arms of Poland, Lithuania and of Queen Elisabeth of Habsburg, the wife of Kazimierz Jagiellończyk. The Baroque interior is noteworthy for the outstanding Cracow carving work from the 17th and 18th centuries, of which the high altar and the choir stalls from the first half of the seventeenth century are excellent examples. The painting of the birth of Jesus in the high altar is the work of Tomaso Dolabella. The paintings in the choir stalls were executed by members of the Dolabella circle and portray scenes from the life of saints of the Order of the Lateran Canons. The stained-glass windows in the choir date from the early 15th century. The altars at the pillars and in the side aisles date from the eighteenth century as does the chancel in the shape of a ship, an unusual, interesting Baroque work of art. Located in the north aisle is a mannerist stone altar (17th c.) with a small coffin which contains the mortal remains of Stanisław Kazimierczyk, who died in 1489 and was revered by the population of Kazimierz. Next to the altar hang votive pictures from the 17th and 18th centuries, which are interesting examples of folk art and an important source of knowledge about the culture and the iconography of Kazimierz. The south aisle contains the Chapel of the Annunciation with a Renaissance painting of the Madonna. Adjacent lies the Gothic St Anne's Chapel with the grave of Bartolomeo Berrecci, who designed the Sigismund Chapel on the Wawel and was councillor in Kazimierz for many years.

Let us now return to Wolnica Square and Krakowska Street. The *Kościół ojców augustianów*/**Augustinian Church** of St Catherine and St Margaret (generally known as St Catherine's) is situated on Skałeczna Street in the direction of the Wawel. In 1363 King Casimir the Great founded this imposing church for the Augustinian Order that had been summoned here from Prague. The edifice, which was not completed until the end of the fourteenth century, was twice destroyed by earthquakes (1443 and 1786). After the partition of Poland the Austrians used the church as a storehouse. It was not until the turn of the nineteenth century that the church was thoroughly restored. Next to the Church of Our Lady this church is one of the most interesting examples of Gothic architecture in Cracow. Clearly visible from the corner of Skałeczna and Augustiańska Street is the chancel, which, surrounded by mighty pier buttresses, appears delicate and slender, underlining the vertical tendencies. On the south side (Skałeczna Street) an atrium was added around the year 1400, which is decorated with beautiful bar tracery and leads into the church. The vaulted ceiling of the atrium is decorated with the coat of arms of Cardinal Zbigniew Oleśnicki. The church is a basilica with a slender, elongated chancel. The high altar contains a painting of the betrothal of St Catherine and the Infant Jesus, created by the

Church on Skałka Hill.

Cracow painter Andrzej Wenesta in 1674. The south aisle contains the interesting mannerist tomb of Wawrzyniec Spytek Jordan and his family, which is presumed to have been erected in the early seventeenth century. To the west the south aisle is adjoined by the St Monica Chapel, also called Hungarian Chapel, today the oratory of the Augustinian nuns. This chapel is only open to the public on 26 April on the occasion of the feast day of Our Lady of the Good Council. The cloister, which surrounds a central monastery garden, borders on the north side of the church. It is decorated with valuable wall paintings from the fourteenth and fifteenth centuries. The best preserved painting, »Christ in the grave«, also known as »Christ in the well«, has been adored by the population of Cracow since the mid-fifteenth century.

The Succour of Mary Chapel, separate from the cloister, contains interesting wall paintings (15th/16th c.), portraying the Madonna with St Augustine and St Nicolas of Tolentino. Adjacent to the chapel lies the mausoleum of the blessed Augustinian monk Izajasz Boner/Jesaja Boner (died 1471). Two further Gothic chapels lie on the east side of the cloister: the Chapel of St Dorothy, whose vault rests on two pillars and which is now used by the Greek-Catholic congregation, and the Chapel of St Thomas, now a sacristy. In the Chapel of St Thomas a single pillar supports the vault on whose keystones you can make out the letters KA-ZI-MI-R, which refer to the founder of the church, Casimir the Great. Also of interest is an iconostasis in the Chapel of St Dorothy, which was a work of the contemporary painter Jerzy Nowosielski.

Leaving the Church of St Catherine, our walk leads along Skałeczna Street towards Skałka Hill, a lime-stone incline opposite Wawel Hill. This beautiful and picturesque spot is connected with the veneration of St Stanislas the Bishop, who according to legend suffered a martyr's death here at the hands of King Bolesław Smiały/Boleslav the Brave in the year 1079. Stanislas was canonized in Assissi in 1253. Since this time many pilgrimages, even some by kings, have been undertaken to **Skałka Hill**. As part of the coronation ritual monarchs had to undertake a pilgrimage to Skałka Hill on the day before the actual coronation.

In the Middle Ages the Church of the Archangel Michael stood on Skałka Hill. First mentioned in the thirteenth century, it was placed in the care of the Pauline Order, which had been summoned here by Jan Długosz, in the second half of the fifteenth century. The present Baroque church, the **Pauline Church**, was built in the second quarter of the eighteenth century and is the work of two architects, namely Anton Gerhardt Müntzer from Brzeg/Brieg, and Antoni Solari, who completed the building work. A monastery adjoins the church to the north. You enter the church complex through a neo-Rococo portal with an ornamental grille (late 19th c.). Located in the forecourt is the rectangular water basin dedicated to St Stanislas, which is furnished with a stone edging, a balustrade, corner obelisks and stairs. Before them stands a Baroque gate with the Korab coat of arms (in Poland the coats of arms of the nobility bear individual names), which refers to Bishop Jakub Zadzik, who donated the gate. On a high pedestal in the middle of the water basin stands a late-Baroque sculpture of St Stanislas. In former times the people of Cracow believed that the water in this basin had healing properties.

Situated in front of the twin-towered facade of the Pauline Church is a monumental double staircase. Between these two sets of stairs lies the entrance to the **Polish Vault of Honour**. The church interior with its homogeneous Baroque furnishings is impressive due to its elegance and, at the same time, its naturalness. The interior was decorated by Johann Georg Lehnert

Augustinian Church of St Catherine's.

and Wojciech Rojowski. The high altar contains a painting of the Archangel Michael by Tadeusz Kuntze. In the chancel, on the left as seen from the entrance, is the Chapel of St Stanislas. Enclosed in the altar is a piece of wood onto which the blood of the holy martyr is said to have fallen. Adjacent stands a bust of Jan Długosz, the benefactor of the Paulinians.

The spacious crypt beneath the church, which was established on the occasion of the 400th anniversary of the death of Jan Długosz (buried on Skałka Hill in 1480), contains the graves of Poles who have rendered outstanding services to their country. After the mortal remains of Jan Długosz had been transferred here in 1880, this national pantheon was opened officially. The Polish Vault of Honour supplements the burial place on the Wawel which is designated for kings, national heroes and poets. The following are amongst those buried on Skałka Hill next to Jan Długosż: Lucjan Siemński, Wincenty Pol, Teofil Lenartowicz, Józef Ignacy Kraszewski, Adam Asnyk, Henryk Siemiradzki, Stanisław Wyspiański, Jacek Malczewski, Karol Szymanowski, Tadeusz Banachiewicz and Ludwik Solski. This burial place for meritorious Poles is one of the places that are frequently visited by the population. On leaving the church you will see a high wall on the garden side, the remains of Kazimierz's old town fortifications. From here you can also see the incomplete brick facade of St Catherine's. Walking along Skałeczna and Krakowska Street we come to ulica Józefa/Joseph Street.

Our walk now leads us to the **Jewish Town** in Kazimierz, the former *Oppidum Judaeorum*, which came into existence in the late 15th century. Before that the Jewish community of Cracow had lived in the area of *ulica św. Anny*/St Anne's Street on the later site of the Cracow Academy. In the 15th century they lived around the present Szczepański Square, until following a decree by King Jan Olbracht/John Albert they were resettled in Kazimierz, where a separate Jewish Town was created following the European example. The buildings that belong to a Jewish community were speedily erected–synagogues, a cemetery (*Kirkut*), a ritual bathing-house (*Mykwa*) and dwelling houses. They took the area around *ulica Szeroka*/Broad Street and built a wall to separate themselves from the Christian section. This state of affairs continued until the early 19th century when the ghetto was dissolved and the population of Jewish descent was allowed to live in the entire area of Kazimierz. Until 1939 the Jewish population mainly lived in Kazimierz and Stradom, where they created a particular cultural, religious and economic climate. Synagogues and Jewish cemeteries were to be found here. This all came to an end with the Nazis, who carried out a bloodbath amongst the Jewish population. On the area of Podgórze, on the right bank of the Weichsel, they established a ghetto. The Jews were either murdered immediately or sent to their deaths in concentration camps. Jewish works of art were destroyed, synagogues torn down, and cemeteries desecrated.

Old Synagogue in Kazimierz.

Located at 38 Joseph Street is the former ***Bożnica Wysoka*/High Synagogue**, which was erected in the second half of the 16th century. On the corner of Jacob and Isaac Street stands the Baroque ***Bożnica Izaaka*/Isaac Synagogue**, which was built before the middle of the 17th century with funds provided by the wealthy merchant Izaak Jakubowicz. Along Isaac Street we come to Kupa Street and the Baroque **Bożnica Kupa/Kupa Synagoge**, however, religious services are no longer held.

The largest complex of old Jewish buildings is to be found on *ulica Szeroka*/**Broad Street**. One of the most interesting edifices is without doubt the ***Stara Synagoga*/Old Synagogue** (24 Broad Street). It was built at the turn of the fifteenth century and has kept its original appearance, though structural alterations were carried out on several occasions. Having been destroyed in a fire, the synagogue was rebuilt in the second half of the sixteenth century by Matteo Gucci and received a rib vault supported by two columns. For centuries it formed the centre of Jewish religious life. After World War II it was restored, and the Jewish department of the Cracow Museum of Town History has been established here. Its collections consist of ritual objects, Jewish mementos and iconographical objects from the Jewish Town. Amongst the most valuable exhibits are, for example, Torah mantles, caps, chanukka candlesticks, and circumcision knives as well as paintings with

83

Jewish themes. Part of the exhibition is dedicated to the martyrdom of the Jews during World War II. Of the original furnishings of the synagogue a stone Thora shrine (Aron Hakodesch) was saved. The beautiful bema, on the other hand, had to be reconstructed after the war. Works of art have been gathered here that bear testimony to the important role and the standing of Jewish artists within Polish culture.

Next to the Old Synagogue stands part of the reconstructed town wall. At 16 Broad Street you will find the *Bożnica Popera*/**Poper Synagogue**, which Wolf Poper (or Bocian), one of the most important Jewish bankers, had built in 1620.

Situated on Broad Street are also the Jewish Cemetery (*Kirkuł*) and the *Bożnica Remu'h*/**Remu'h Synagogue**, which is still in use. Donated by Izrael Isserles, the king's financial advisor, it was built in the second half of the sixteenth century. Around the synagogue lies the old Jewish *cmentarz Remu'h*/**Remu'h Cemetery**, on which you will find many Renaissance and Baroque gravestones. Behind the church, beneath a tree with outstretched branches lies a striking tomb which is closed off by railings. It is the tomb of the scholarly Rabbi Moses Isserles, who was called Rabbi Moses-Remu'h. He was the son of the donator of the synagogue, and his contemporaries as well as later generations believed that he could work miracles. From all over the world Jews come to his grave to pray, and leave cards with pleas and expressions of gratitude. Amongst Jews there is the belief and the conviction that the graves of religious scholars are close to God and that the deceased can convey pleas and requests to Yahweh.

The little cards on Remu'h's grave are a special feature of this Jewish cemetery, which has a unique atmosphere, reinforced by the absolute silence of this spot.

From the Remu'h Cemetery and Synagogue we return to Broad Street and the little public garden surrounded by a low railing decorated with Jewish motifs. This, too, is a Jewish cemetery. According to legend, a wedding party had once been held into the late hours of a Friday night, although the Sabbath had already begun and a Rabbi had expressed a warning. As punishment all the wedding guests died, and were buried together in a communal grave, around which a wall was then built. Another story tells that an unhappy newly-wed couple was buried here. It is said that since this time no Jewish wedding has taken place on a Friday in Cracow. You will find similar stories and also alleged graves of young couples in many Jewish communities in the eastern border regions of the old Poland. Scholem An-Ski used this motif in

Remu'h Cemetery in Kazimierz.

»Dybuk«. At 6 Broad Street stands the recently restored building of a large Jewish bathing-house with a water basin that is fed by running spring water.

From Broad Street we enter the *ulica Miodowa*/Honey Street, and at its corner with Podbrzezie Street there stands the **Temple Synagogue**, which was built at the beginning of the second half of the nineteenth century and belonged to the Society of Progressive Jews. It was famous for its services with an extended liturgy, and for the singing and the sermons, which were held in Polish and in German by academically trained speakers. The innovations introduced here provoked protest and indignation amongst the orthodox Jews who prayed in the other synagogues in Kazimierz. The interior of the great hall was ornamented with stucco work, stylized patterns on the walls and interesting stained-glass windows. The hall is surrounded by the women's gallery, which rests on ornamented columns. The bema stands in the centre, and the Thora shrine made of white marble at the east wall.

On 24 October 1990 a concert was held here with the theme of Polish-Jewish reconciliation. This occasion was commemorated with a new Star of David on the wall.

Here we leave the Cracow district of Kazimierz, which has lost the unique atmosphere that the Jewish community, who regarded Kazimierz as their holy town, as *»mein sztetl«*, gave it.

Daniłowicz shaft in the salt mine in Wieliczka.

Excursions

Nowa Huta

If you have some spare time, then visiting Cracow's surroundings, which are now incorporated into the region of Greater Cracow, is to be recommended. Near Nowa Huta, a part of Cracow built after the war, lies the old village of Mogiła, which is worth visiting for its fifteenth-century wooden parish church of St Bartholomew (structurally altered in the 18th c.). In the centre of the village stands a mighty Cistercian Abbey (Klasztorna Street). The Cistercian Church dates from the first half of the thirteenth century, and was consecrated in the second half of the thirteenth century. It was Bishop Iwo Odrowąż who summoned the Cistercians to Mogiła.

The church was erected on the outline of a Latin cross as a basilica with pairs of so-called twin chapels that surround the choir. Though rebuilt several times, the church has kept its early-Gothic character. The plain late-Baroque facade dates from the second half of the eighteenth century. The nave and the aisles are decorated with ornamental wall paintings by Jan Bukowski (early twentieth century). The choir, the transept and the cloister, on the other hand, contain Renaissance wall paintings by Stanisław Samostrzelnik, a Cistercian monk from Mogiła who is considered the most important Polish painter of the Renaissance. The high altar is a late-Gothic polyptych; the stained-glass windows were made after World War II according to designs by Tadeusz Wojciechowski, and blend in well with the medieval architecture. The Chapel of the Crucified Christ, located in the north arm of the transept, is closed off by a Baroque grille. The monastery with the cloister adjoins the church to the south. An early-Gothic (thirteenth century) portal forms the entrance to the church from the cloister. The monastery gardens are also worth visiting, as from there you have a good view of the structure of the early-Gothic choir.

Not far from the Cistercian Abbey you can see the Wanda Hill, which rises above the valley of a little river. According to legend, this hill is said to be the grave of the daughter of the legendary Prince Krak. Presumably, the hill was artificially made in the seventh century for either ritual or signalling purposes. On the summit stands a monument designed by Jan Matejko, who owned

89

Interior of the church in Mistrzejowice.

a little estate in the former village of Krzesławice (today situated at 15 Wańkowicz Street). Several years ago the estate became the property of the Society of the Friends of Fine Arts, which organised an exhibition commemorating the artist Matejko. Another of their achievements has been to reconstruct the original furnishings of the house.

In the vicinity of Nowa Huta there are two good examples of modern sacral architecture, namely the churches in the former villages of Bieńczyce and Mistrzejowice.

In Bieńczyce you will find a church dedicated to the Virgin Mary, the Queen of Poland, and designed by Wojciech Pietrzyk as a monument to the thousandth anniversary of the Christianization of Poland. The foundation stone of the church came from the grave of St Peter in Rome and was a gift of Pope Paul VI. This unique building, which bears resemblance to an ark – hence its name »Ark of the Lord«– was consecrated in the year 1977 by Cardinal Karol Wojtyła. Near the altar you will find an expressive sculpture of

»Ark of the Lord« Church in Nowa Huta.

Christ on the Cross, the work of Bronisław Chromy. In a subterranean chapel you can visit the so-called »Polish pietà portrayals« by Antoni Rząsa from Zakopane. They depict the martyrdom that the Polish people had to endure during the Second World War.

From Bieńczyce it is not far to Mistrzejowice, where another interesting church, the Church of St Maximilian Maria Kolbe, was built a few years ago to a design by Józef Dutkiewicz. In its interior you will find a sculpture of the Crucified Christ between the Madonna and St Maximilian Maria Kolbe. It is the work of the Warsaw sculptor Gustaw Zemła, who also created the cloisters and the interior of the Maltese Chapel of St John the Baptist, which was donated by the Ciechanowieckis and lies to the right of the entrance.

Pope John Paul II himself consecrated this church in the year 1983. A statue of him stands in front of the church, also the work of Zemła.

Benedictine Abbey in Tyniec.

Wieliczka

The town of Wieliczka lies about 12 kilometres east of Cracow on the road to Tarnów. Situated here is one of the oldest salt mines, which was in extensive use from the thirteenth century on. The underground passages are over 150 kilometres long. The mine in Wieliczka formerly brought in substantial returns and the power of the Polish kings mainly rested on this »salty treasure«, which was also responsible for Cracow's development. Part of the now exhausted mine and also a unique Salt Mining Museum are now open to visitors, who are fascinated by the mysterious world of salt chapels, chambers, tunnels, salt lakes and figures sculpted out of salt, by the subterranean Chapel of the Blessed Kinga/Kunigunde and also by the ancient mining installations, which bear testimony to the high standard of the mine. The museum part illustrates the history of mining in Wieliczka; on display are items such as miners' clothing and equipment, documents, privileges and plans of the mine. As the micro-climate of the mine has a therapeutic effect, a sanatorium for illnesses of the respiratory tract as well as for certain allergies has been established here. In 1978 the UNESCO included the Wieliczka Salt Mine in its list of the world's cultural heritage.

Palace in Pieskowa Skała.

Niepołomice

Not far from Cracow, pleasantly located on the river Weichsel, lies the little town of Niepołomice, a former royal hunting and summer seat on the edge of the Niepołomicka Heath, an ancient hunting area. Here you will find a royal palace in Renaissance style complete with an arcaded courtyard, as well as a parish church, which was founded by King Casimir the Great. Amongst its most interesting features are the mannerist Branicki Chapel (presumed to be the work of Santi Gucci), the early-Baroque Lubomirski Chapel (first half of the 17th c.) and the medieval wall paintings in the so-called Old Sacristy (second half of the 14th c.). A reserve for the European bison (wisent) has been established in the Niepołomicka Heath. Over the centuries Niepołomice witnessed many historical events and meetings of rulers. The Piast and Jagiellon monarchs came here to relax and to hunt. Before the Battle of Grunwald large hunts took place on the heath, and King Władysław Jagiełło stayed here after his victory on his way back to Cracow. Both Zygmunt I Stary/Sigismund I the Old and Zygmunt August/Sigismund Augustus stayed here frequently. Niepołomice's importance declined, however, after the royal seat was transferred to Warsaw.

Tyniec

The Benedictine Abbey in Tyniec is picturesquely situated on a lime-stone hill on the bank of the river Weichsel. A road leads from the market square in the town district of Dębniki directly to the abbey. The origins of Tyniec go back to the time of the very first Piasts, and scholars still argue about who its founder was. The monastery, which was founded by King Bolesław Śmiały/Boleslav the Brave, was built in the second half of the eleventh century. Very quickly it became a centre of spiritual and cultural life. In the fifteenth and seventeenth centuries the church was fundamentally rebuilt. The abbey was badly damaged by Russian soldiers during the Confederation of Bar, and deteriorated further during the nineteenth century. Rebuilding work was not begun until after World War II. The Church of Sts Peter and Paul was rebuilt in Baroque style in the early seventeenth century. Worth looking at are the early-Baroque paintings in the choir stalls, the late-Baroque high altar (presumably designed by Francesco Placidi) and also fragments of eleventh-century Romanesque architecture in the cloister. On the church courtyard you should take a look at the wooden well-house, now a rare cultural monument from the Baroque age.

From the square in front of the Benedictine Monastery you have a lovely view onto the *Las Wolski*/Wolski Forest. On the horizon you can also see the outline of the Camaldolese Church in Bielany, which was built in the seventeenth century by the architect Andrea Spezza with funds donated by the magnate Mikołaja Wolski.

Ojców

The extended surroundings of Cracow have attracted tourists for a long time, as you can find numerous picturesque landscape regions of differing character here. Ojców and the Ojców National Park lie in the valley of the river Prądnik, approximately 25 kilometres north of Cracow. Deep caves and botanical rarities, such as the Ojców birch, are hidden amongst the Jurassic lime-stone rocks and thick forests. Of the lime-stone caves the *Jaskinia Ciemna*/Dark Cave and the *Grota Łokietka*/Łokietek's Grotto deserve particular mention. According to centuries-old tradition, the Polish king Władysław Łokietek/Ladislav the Short is said to have hidden from his enemies in the *Grota Łokietka* during the battles for the

Bernardine Church in Kalwaria Zebrzydowska.

unity of the Polish state. In Ojców you will also find the remains of a medieval castle which recall the days of Casimir the Great. The castle, which stands high above the Prądnik Valley, lies on the so-called »Path of the Eagles' Nests«. Worth visiting is also the National Museum, named after Prof. Wladysław Szafer and located in the Villa Łokietek.

Pieskowa Skała

A few kilometres north of Ojców, next to the so-called Hercules Cudgel, stands the Renaissance palace in Pieskowa Skała– originally a medieval royal border fortress, which was later turned into the imposing residence of the families Szafraniec, Zabrzydowski and Wielopolski. Today it houses a section of the State Art Collections on the Wawel, in which unusually interesting examples of domestic interiors from the Middle Ages to the nineteenth century can be seen. In addition to splendid furniture, porcelain, silver and sculptures the collection encompasses paintings by Old Masters. The walls of the palace are hung with valuable tapestries of French, Flemish and Dutch provenance. They include a series depicting scenes from the life of Alexander the Great which was commissioned by Franciszek Salezy Potocki, and made in Aubusson. When visiting the palace you should particularly note the pillared arcaded courtyard, which the Szafraniecs had rebuilt in the second half of the sixteenth century. One of the Baroque bastions has been turned into a stylish café and a restaurant.

Kalwaria Zebrzydowska

Kalwaria Zebrzydowska, which lies approx. 35 kilometres southeast of Cracow, possesses a Bernardine monastery, founded in the early seventeenth century by the Cracow Wojewode Mikolaj Zebrzydowski. The shrine to the Virgin Mary in the Baroque church has attracted many pilgrims, amongst them Pope John Paul II. Located southeast of the monastery on picturesque hills and in small valleys lies a Mount Calvary, consisting of the small churches and the small and tiny chapels of the Stations of the Cross and the Passion of Mary. Well-known passion plays take place here during Holy Week, as well as celebrations on the Stations of the Life of Mary around 15 August, Assumption Day. The mystery plays form an unforgettable religious experience.